# Sweet Soul

# Sweet Soul

A Biography of Rabbi Isaiah "Shy" Zeldin

PAUL J. CITRIN

*Foreword by Yoshi Zweiback*

*Afterword by Eli Herscher*

RESOURCE *Publications* · Eugene, Oregon

SWEET SOUL
A Biography of Rabbi Isaiah "Shy" Zeldin

Resource Publications
An Imprint of Wipf and Stock Publishers
199 W. 8th Ave., Suite 3
Eugene, OR 97401

www.wipfandstock.com

PAPERBACK ISBN: 979-8-3852-6201-4
HARDCOVER ISBN: 979-8-3852-6202-1
EBOOK ISBN: 979-8-3852-6203-8

VERSION NUMBER 102325

Dedicated to the clergy, professional staff and members of Stephen S. Wise Temple who helped make Shy's dreams a reality.

*In Yiddish, we say, "Er hut a zisse neshameh" (This person has a sweet soul). Your soul that I don't know and that I cannot see exists just as much as your physical attributes. That soul, your n'shamah, is what life is all about. The cultivation of each person's n'shamah is essentially the challenge of human existence.*

—Rabbi Isaiah Zeldin
Quoted from a marginal comment in the
Stephen S. Wise *High Holy Day Machzor.*

# Contents

# Foreword

Rabbi Yoshi Zweiback

I ONCE ASKED RABBI Isaiah Zeldin—Shy as he was affectionately known—how he built Stephen Wise Temple and its schools. The undertaking required extraordinary effort. Tens of millions of dollars had to be raised. Multiple campuses were developed, and dozens of buildings constructed, each demanding countless hours of work with architects, construction companies and building committees. At the same time, he continued doing the work of a congregational rabbi: baby naming, bar and bat mitzvahs, weddings, funerals, Shabbat and holiday services, and educational programs.

How did he do it all?

He paused for a moment and then said without a hint of self-pity: "Every single weeknight, over the course of a few decades, I was out to dinner with a congregant or potential donor. There were lunches and coffees and parlor meetings. Many nights away from my family. It never stopped."

That relentless dedication—to his community, to Jewish education and more broadly, to the Jewish people—was the essence of who Shy was. There are many leaders who can articulate inspiring visions for the future. But there are few with the determination, grit, and yes, *chutzpah,* to make those visions a reality.

Rabbi Isaiah Zeldin dreamed great dreams—and then did the hard work to bring them to fruition.

This beautifully crafted portrait of Rabbi Zeldin offers readers a window into the life of a man who inspired generations of students, colleagues and lay leaders. Those of us blessed to call him our teacher, mentor or friend knew his brilliance, his fierce love for our people, and his unshakeable belief in the power of Jewish education.

The other central focus of his rabbinate was his enduring love for Israel. Shy saw in the modern State of Israel both a miracle and a responsibility—a place where the Jewish story could unfold with freedom and dignity.

These two passions—Jewish education and Israel—were rooted in his expansive vision of Jewish community. Shy loved people deeply and welcomed them warmly into every circle he led—from the grand institutions he built to the humble Shabbat dinners he hosted at Wendy's in Palm Desert in his final years.

A builder of communities, schools, synagogues, institutions and relationships—Shy was, in the end, proudest of his most personal legacy: his family. For them and for all who were touched by him, Shy's life will remain a blessing.

# 1

## Prologue

SHY IS THE FURTHEST conceivable adjective one could attach to Rabbi Isaiah Zeldin. He was outgoing and thoroughly a people person. So where did his nickname, "Shy," come from? His name, Yishayahu, in Hebrew, yielded the name "Shy." Family, long-time friends, and synagogue leaders called him Shy. They did so with great affection and deep connection.

Rabbi Isaiah "Shy" Zeldin loved to quote the book of Proverbs, "Let another praise you, not your own mouth." (Proverbs 27:2) Then, he would take mischievous delight in rephrasing the verse this way: Let others praise you, but *if not*, your own mouth. Shy had no problem, privately or publicly, praising his own successes and those of Stephen S. Wise Temple. What he did broadcast was not driven by ego. When he talked about what he, his staff, and the congregation accomplished, Shy sought to excite a community to participate in temple life.

Shy had every reason to allow his own mouth to praise his accomplishments. Stephen S. Wise Temple was his conception, his dream. He concretized it as a full-service synagogue center in Los Angeles and made it live. No one else could see the Temple community with quite the fullness that Shy did. He created an institution that is unique in North America and around the world. In

SWEET SOUL

the pages to come, we will look at the components that went into
conceiving and building Stephen S. Wise Temple.

We will look at Shy's background to learn what shaped him.
Shy had the ability to recruit able and supportive lay leaders. He
was a master fundraiser, accumulating hundreds of millions of
dollars for congregational projects and buildings. Along the way,
he helped donors enjoy giving and participating.

Shy was aided in substantial ways by his wife, Florence Karp
Zeldin. Her warmth and genuineness, her creativity and intelligence bolstered his gifts. They raised together two fine sons, Joel,
an attorney in San Francisco, and Michael, a professor of education
at the Hebrew Union College in Los Angeles. Being at the helm of
a large Los Angeles congregation (over three thousand families at
its high point) was as taxing as it was exciting. Florence and Shy
still managed to be excellent parents. The proof of the parenting
is in the character and quality of Joel, Michael, and their families.
We will take note of the threads and themes of Zeldin's family life
going back to Shy's parents.

In Eastern Europe, a child or a young teen who mastered
vast amounts of Biblical and Talmudic learning was called an *illuy*. The word, whose root means to ascend, suggests that such a
student is academically above his peers, a prodigy. As a student,
Shy was an *illuy*, absorbing and retaining a panoply of traditional
texts. As a teacher, Shy would present ancient material to address
contemporary issues in a relevant way. He critically analyzed texts
that he taught. Shy modeled superb teaching, inspiring students,
enabling them to achieve their potential in Jewish learning and
embody Jewish values.

Shy was admired by other rabbis who asked his advice as well
as by lay people. In Europe, such a rabbi was sometimes called a
*Gaon*, a contemporary Hebrew word for genius. Reform Jews do
not look for a *Gaon* in Jewish law because, as Mordecai Kaplan
said, we allow Jewish law a voice but not a veto. Yet we may consider Shy Zeldin a true *Gaon* for our times. He had imagination and
the ability to translate vision into action and to obtain institutional

realities. He motivated others, led by example, and encouraged the talents of other people. At community building, he was a *Gaon*.

Shy was an eloquent spokesman for issues of social justice. As a fierce defender of the Jewish people and of the State of Israel, he was sought out by several Israeli Prime Ministers and other senior government officials who knew of Shy and of Stephen S. Wise Temple. He spoke out for Soviet Jews who were denied Judaism and the freedom to leave the Soviet Union. He embodied the verse from the prophet Isaiah, "For Zion's sake I will not be still" (Isaiah 62:1).

The pages ahead will pursue in depth the influences and experiences that shaped Shy Zeldin and which modeled his ability to guide others. The goal of this biography is to learn what made Shy Zeldin a *Gedol Hador*, one of the great rabbis of his twentieth-century generation.

# 2

# Shy and This Biographer

On a Friday in April 1963, after I arrived home from school, our phone rang. I answered; it was Rabbi Zeldin calling.

"Paulie," so he often called me, "are you coming to Services this evening?"

"Yes, Rabbi. We are planning to be there."

"Then please come and see me in my study about fifteen minutes before Services begin around 7:45."

"Okay, Rabbi, I'll come by."

My parents and I went into Rabbi Zeldin's study right on time.

Rabbi Zeldin wished us Shabbat Shalom and got right to the point.

"Paulie, how would you like to go to Israel this summer?"

I could not believe what I heard. I had loved Israel and wanted to go there since the age of nine. My Hebrew teacher, Metuka Miliken (now Benjamin), had indoctrinated me with tales of her girlhood in British Palestine and in the early days of the State of Israel. Somehow, I had the presence of mind to respond this way to my rabbi.

"I would love to go to Israel, but I don't want to just meet waiters and busboys. I want to be involved in Israeli life."

"Don't worry. We will find a kibbutz that takes in volunteers over the summer. You can go and be part of kibbutz life."

I was ecstatic and all the more excited when Rabbi Zeldin told my parents and me that he had a five-hundred-dollar scholarship for me to make this trip a reality. I left Los Angeles in June of 1963 for ten weeks at Kibbutz Dovrat for farm work, learning conversational Hebrew, and touring the country. I came home to my senior year strong and healthy, fluent in everyday Hebrew, and full of the spirit of Israel.

It so happened that on the day I left Los Angeles for Israel via Idlewild airport (now JFK), Shy and Florence were in Brooklyn visiting family. They met me at the airport and took me to Katz's Deli for a pre-departure dinner. Between the pastrami sandwich, the gruff waiter, and the cultural experience, I was in paradise. This hospitality of the Zeldins was another example of their going the extra distance of outreach and caring. Because I had never traveled beyond San Francisco, and certainly not overseas on my own, the Zeldins' presence and attention bolstered me for my adventure.

I have begun telling what Shy did for me with the Israel scholarship because it was a high point among his many efforts to open doors for me and to guide me. He gave of himself to other students as well. On Shabbat mornings, seventy-five minutes before Services, Shy taught modern Hebrew to me, to his son, Joel, and to two other students. The burden of that weekly commitment was sustained by Shy's devotion to Hebrew education and to Israel.
I remember a few times when Shy would pick me up from my house to take me to his home in the San Fernando Valley to get together with his son, Joel. Shy dropped us off at Joe Palooka's bowling alley for the afternoon. I enjoyed a special personal relationship with Shy and his family. When Shy blessed me in front of the Ark at my Bar Mitzvah, I felt a warm and golden glow enveloping me.

Rabbi Zeldin taught the tenth-grade Confirmation class. He was a captivating teacher who garnered the attention of most of us teen students. As always, there were a few disinterested troublemakers. Rabbi Zeldin managed them with a soft but stern voice and a penetrating look. One afternoon between class sessions, Rabbi Zeldin took me aside. "Paulie, you will be the Valedictorian at the Confirmation Service."

I demurred. "There are smarter kids than me who got better scores on your test."

"No, you will be the Valedictorian, and you will give a talk on the book of Proverbs from which we read at Confirmation."

The honor he gave to me was thus sealed, as was my task for explicating Proverbs to the congregation assembled.

In 1964, my senior year of high school, I served as the youth group president at Temple Emanuel. I was also hired as a Hebrew teacher for beginning students. In February, the ongoing disagreements and friction between Rabbi Zeldin and the board reached an eruption point. Shy resigned from the pulpit of Temple Emanuel of Beverly Hills. The rabbi's exit was an earthquake to the congregation. My parents, among others, resolved to leave Temple Emanuel. Since my parents made it clear that they were in the camp supporting Rabbi Zeldin, the Executive Director, and the youth group advisor told me that because of my parents' position, I could no longer serve as youth group president. The Hebrew school principal fired me as a teacher for the same reason. When Rabbi Zeldin got wind of my dual expulsions, he called me immediately. He wanted to know the details of my battles with the powers at Emanuel. He listened intently and asked questions. He was empathetic and supportive. I felt heard and glad to be on his team.

Rabbi Zeldin founded Stephen S. Wise Temple in the spring of 1964. Thirty-five families, including my own, were the founding nucleus with him. The rabbi secured the use of the sanctuary and social hall of St. Alban Episcopal Church across from U.C.L.A. on Hilgard Avenue. The first Service drew four hundred people: the curious, the seekers, and the committed. There was an electric, pioneering excitement and a deep sense of community that was palpable each Friday evening in the church.

In 1965, when I was a freshman at U.C.L.A., Shy once again opened an experiential gateway for me. He invited me to speak at a Friday evening Service. I reviewed Isaac Bashevis Singer's book, *In My Father's Court*. Though I was a bit nervous to be on the bimah, my words were well chosen and fluent. I found I had a knack for public speaking, and I enjoyed it.

Many years later, in 2002, Shy and Florence retired in Palm Desert Sun City. They attended Services on a Friday evening at my Palm Desert congregation, Temple Sinai. I delivered a sermon without notes, just as Shy always did. After the Service, Shy said to me, "Your personality really comes across when you're on the bimah." His words touched my heart, and I reminded him of the start he gave me decades previously at St. Alban.

There were other times over the years when Shy went to bat for me or put opportunities in my path. Rabbi Alexander Segel, ordained by the Hebrew Union College in 1918, retired in Los Angeles. He wanted to donate his rabbinic library to Stephen S. Wise Temple. Rabbi Zeldin asked me to pick up the boxes of books from the Rabbi and bring them to the Temple. As a reward for my effort and to encourage my own studies, Shy told me to take for my own small but increasing Judaica library whatever books I wanted. Thus, I acquired as a first-year rabbinic student (1964–65) volumes of midrash, the full Shulchan Aruch, a concordance to the Bible, and other useful volumes. I cherish the books as Shy knew I would. They remain in my library in use.

Another opportunity Shy put in my path came about when I dropped into his office while I was visiting Los Angeles. In the course of our conversation, Shy offered me a position on the rabbinic staff of the congregation. The idea of working with him and with his dynamic professional team seriously caught my attention. Then I remembered I had just signed a new contract with my current congregation. I had to decline Shy's flattering offer.

In 1996, I accepted the position of senior rabbi of Main Line Reform Temple in Wynnewood, PA., a nearby suburb of Philadelphia. Within the first six months of my tenure, I realized I had made a career mistake by engaging with that congregation. My predecessor was passive and asked little of the Board. The Board was simply not prepared for me, an activist rabbi who learned the principles of a strong rabbinic tenure from Shy Zeldin. My situation reminded me of what I knew of Shy's experience thirty years earlier at Temple Emanuel. I called Shy to discuss my situation. I told him that I would remain as the rabbi of the congregation through the second year of my three-year contract and then depart. I told him I would like to get back to the West in any case. Shy told me of a fairly new and growing congregation in Las Vegas, Nevada, which was seeking a rabbi. Shy had connections in that congregation and felt I would have a good chance of being called to the community. Nonetheless, neither my wife nor I could envision living in the Nevada desert. Shy tried hard to encourage me, but I declined. The irony is that we ended up moving from Philadelphia to Palm Desert, California. Shy and Florence eventually retired there.

My last major pulpit was Congregation Beth Israel in San Diego, California. I invited Shy to install me on the first Friday evening in July 2004. In his inimitable way, he warmed the congregation with a couple of stories. He said some nice words about me as well. Then, he spoke of the accomplishments of Stephen S. Wise Temple as the fully realized embodiment of a synagogue-community center. The purpose of his remarks was to put the congregation on notice that if they would support the dreams and visions of the new rabbi, Beth Israel would flourish. At my installation, I recalled doing some nitty-gritty work to help create Stephen S. Wise Temple.

To build Stephen S. Wise Temple on the property that the congregation purchased in 1964 on Mulholland Drive, the signatures of neighbors were required to move ahead with building permits. Shy did not leave the collection of signatures only to his lay leaders. He himself took the petition on a clipboard and rang neighboring doorbells. He invited me to walk the area with him, which I was pleased to do as a young college student. When a neighbor answered the door, Shy introduced himself as, of course, the Rabbi of Stephen S. Wise Temple. He greeted people with a friendliness and warmth that put them at ease. He explained the project. He brought his lifelong enthusiasm to bear. He convincingly answered questions to the satisfaction of those who initially hesitated to sign. In the end, the Temple, with Shy's shoulder to the wheel, received the necessary signatures to break ground. Walking with Shy as he met and spoke with neighbors was another advanced lesson through role modeling of reaching out to people and bringing them close.

I continued for the next sixty years to bask in Shy's light. Though he died in 2018, his presence shines in my heart and mind. The warmth of his caring personality and the ardent flame of his dynamic creativity illumine my path to this day. For these reasons, I have undertaken to write his biography. It is my hope, through this biography, to keep alive his values, efforts, and achievements. The members of Wise Temple today surely have heard of the founding rabbi, but it is important that they know who he was as an exemplary Jewish leader and visionary. If each of us takes a piece of Shy's positive, confident attitude, belief in one's capabilities, firm ethical convictions, and love of the Jewish people and Israel, Shy's spirit will live among us, pointing to a future filled with Jewish hope.

*Vision looks inward and becomes duty.*
*Vision looks outward and becomes aspiration.*
*Vision looks upward and becomes faith.*

—RABBI STEPHEN S. WISE

# 3

# A Father's Influence

IN 1969, A PLAY entitled "Once There Was a Hasid" opened in Tel Aviv. The play was a series of vignettes that told stories of Jewish life in the Pale of Settlement (Lithuania, Volhynia, Podolia, and White Russia). One story opens with a mother begging her young son not to go to the barn at night lest he be grabbed by a "Khopper," a Jew who snatched pre-adolescents and young teens for the Czar's army. The Jews were compelled to provide a certain number of soldiers to the army, even if that meant kidnapping them. The term of army service was twenty-five years, counting from the conscript's nineteenth birthday, even though he might have been seized at age twelve. The goal of this cruel and lengthy conscription was to erase from young Jews any memory of Jewish practice and identity.

The boy in the vignette tells his mother not to worry. He says he will milk the goat and then return to her in the house. But a khopper is hiding in the barn. He grabs the boy and takes him away. After twenty-five years, the boy, who has now grown into a man, old before his time, comes home to his mother's house. He kisses the mezuzah and enters the house. His mother, wrapped in a blanket and sitting in her chair, is shocked, nearly catatonic, when she sees him come in. The son says to her, "Why are you shocked, Mother? I told you I would return." This statement is full of emotion, which demonstrates the determination to remain an identifying Jew.

This story is based on the 1827 ukase (decree) of Czar Nicholas I (1825–1855) to conscript Jewish boys for a quarter of a century. Czar Alexander II (1855–1878) continued his father's intention to Russify the Jews. His government opposed cheder (Jewish elementary schools) and Yeshivot (Jewish schools of higher learning). Nevertheless, there were Jewish intellectuals who rejected Russification. They emphasized Jewish learning. They valued and taught Hebrew and wrote literary works in Hebrew. They continued the Enlightenment started by Western European Jews but with a new, intense focus on Jewish culture and peoplehood.

In 1874, the twenty-five-year military conscription was abolished. From that point on, there would be general military conscription for all males, including Jews. This new structure gave Jews comparable obligations to their gentile fellow soldiers, but Jews did not have privileges equal to theirs.

Although military requirements upon Jews were gradually eased, they were far from abolished by 1891, the year that Moishe Zeldin was born in Petrokov, a town in the Minsk district. Moishe came from a family of Torah scholars. It was natural for him to follow their path. He was a quick student absorbing vast amounts of Talmud and Halacha (rabbinic law). Family lore claims that he was ordained a rabbi at age fourteen. His yeshiva could well have recognized his learning by declaring him a Rav (Rabbi) based on the knowledge he garnered. He had acquired the tools to teach and to render halachic decisions. What is less likely is that at his age, he would be much consulted. His learning, however, would sustain him in the United States in years to come.

Moishe Zeldin was drafted into the Russian army at fifteen or sixteen years old. It was not an environment that appreciated Jewish troops nor their Orthodox customs and ritual requirements. Moishe detested the military. He not only recoiled from the treif (non-kosher) food served to him but also from having to receive it in the front of his shirttail rather than on a mess kit dish.

Moishe's father attempted to obtain for him an exemption from military service. Moishe did so by drinking quantities of vinegar to try to induce a heart condition or another grave illness. Not only did the plan fail to work, but it turned out that only gentile boys could get an exemption for family reasons. Moishe did manage to get a pass for a short leave. He returned home. While Moishe was in his natal village, he learned that a young man of similar age by the name of Lifschitz had recently died. Lifschitz had obtained a document that would allow him to travel. Moishe was given the document by the family. In 1907, he made a four-month journey by foot to the German port city of Hamburg.

Moishe arrived in the United States in January 1908. He took the American name Morris, and that is the name we will use in the pages to come. He landed in Baltimore and continued to Rochester, New York, eventually settling in Brooklyn.

There is a folktale about travelers aboard a ship who debate whose cargo is worth the most. After listening to the competitive bragging, one man who had been quiet stated that he had cargo beyond all their riches. The others asked him to show them what he had. He said it was hidden. The others searched the ship and found nothing. When there arose a storm off the coast of a nearby country, the ship took on water and sank. The passengers made it to shore, but their merchandise was lost. They had nothing to sustain them where they landed. Only the man who said his cargo was hidden managed to earn an income in the new land, as he was a Torah scholar. He taught students, children, and adults. The other travelers realized that, in fact, Torah is the most precious merchandise.[1]

When Morris Zeldin arrived in the United States, he was loaded with the cargo of Torah. He took a position as a Hebrew teacher. He taught Hebrew *in Hebrew*, a rare endeavor at that time. Soon, he was called to be the principal of a Talmud Torah school.

In Brooklyn, Morris met Esther Shlapochnik, who arrived in the United States in 1911. She was sponsored by a cousin whose family name was Freedman. Esther took on his name and became

1. Based on M. Buber's rendition of this story from Tanchuma

Esther Freedman. Esther and Morris intended to marry, but he threw a challenge her way. He told her that he wanted their children to be raised in a Hebrew-speaking household. Morris said he would marry her only when she learned to speak Hebrew. Esther did not shrink from that goal, nor did she let Morris off the marital hook. She took a Hebrew tutor and learned to speak passable everyday Hebrew in six weeks. The Zeldin home became a Hebrew-speaking home. Their three sons, Jack, Shy, and Bernie, spoke Hebrew before they learned English from their neighbor kids.

Morris, in addition to being an educator, was a person of strong opinions, which he frequently expressed in the Yiddish and Hebrew press in Brooklyn. He was fiery and eloquent in both languages on numerous topics of Jewish concern. In one of his articles, Morris blasted certain Orthodox rabbis who burned the newly published prayerbook of Rabbi Mordecai Kaplan's Reconstructionist movement. Morris condemned the burning of books as medieval, something that Jews never do.

Morris was personally a committed and observant Orthodox Jew. Yet, he apparently had an enlightened view of the role of religion in human society. There are stories that Shy Zeldin used to tell about Morris that suggest his openness to liberal forms of Judaism.

Once, a neighbor in Brooklyn saw Morris in the street. He said to Morris, "Mr. Zeldin, I saw in the paper that a young man named Shy Zeldin will attend rabbinic school by the Reforms at Hebrew Union College. Is he related to you?" Morris said, "Yes, he's my son." The man said to Morris, "You mean he is going to daven (pray in the Orthodox fashion) without a kipah (head covering)?" Morris answered, "Who says he's going to daven!"

Was Morris poking at Reform Judaism or sticking it to a nosey neighbor's implied criticism? Probably, it was both. Yet it was Morris who encouraged Shy to attend Hebrew Union College. He felt Reform congregations treated their rabbis better than did Conservative or Orthodox congregations. In Shy's later years, he said aloud that he never viewed himself as a Reform rabbi but rather as a traditionalist steeped in Judaism. He thought irrational parts of Jewish practice should be removed. He deemed that the extra service on Shabbat, the Musaf in remembrance of the additional Shabbat sacrifice, was not meaningful. He also held the view that the Conservative movement, which was shrinking, would not long survive. Shy would have liked to have seen mergers between Reform and Conservative congregations. He blamed the Conservatives for blocking such efforts.

There is a story from Shy's early days as an assistant rabbi in Newark, New Jersey. His secretary called Shy to tell him that his father was downstairs in the lobby. The lobby had a number of glass display cases with various ritual items in them. The largest one had a full-size, open, and spread-out tallis (prayer shawl) in it. As Shy came down to the lobby, Morris said to him, "I see by you Reform Jews, a tallis is already a museum piece." It was a zinger aimed at Reform Judaism.

On another occasion, Morris attended Shy's congregation on Shabbat. He had to ride to the temple but insisted on parking half a mile away and continuing on foot to maintain the spirit of Shabbat. When Morris arrived at the temple, the Sisterhood Gift Shop was open. Shy hurried to his father to apologize for not having the Gift Shop closed. Morris' response was to say to Shy that if Jews buy ritual items to celebrate the tradition, such purchases would be acceptable on Shabbat.

The understanding and love between father and son prevailed until Morris's death in 1976. Despite Morris' Orthodox way of life, he understood changes in the religious outlook of younger generations.

Morris was not among the most radical Orthodox circles that rejected Zionism and the re-establishment of a Jewish homeland in Eretz Yisrael. He was an ardent and devoted Zionist. Here is a delightful example of how Zionism penetrated to his very bones.

When he was finishing the process of applying for U.S. citizenship in 1919, authorities asked for his birthdate. Morris answered, "Shabbos Breishis."[2] When the gentile administrator

---

2. Jews in eastern Europe referred to their birthdate in relationship to a festival or to the Torah portion of the week. Morris' answer was traditional—he was born on the first Sabbath of Genesis.

gave him a blank look, Morris realized he needed a date on the Western calendar. He changed his answer to November 2nd, the same date as the British government authorized the Balfour Declaration, which affirmed the U.K.'s support for a Jewish homeland in Palestine. While November 2nd was not his actual birthday, the hope that the Balfour Declaration gave all Zionists breathed life and purpose into him.

Whatever occasional wry or sarcastic comments Morris made toward Reform Judaism, the brilliance of certain Reform rabbinic leaders was clear to him. He admired Abba Hillel Silver, Judah Magnes, and Stephen S. Wise. Zionists all, they were leaders of eloquence and stature among North American Jewry. When Stephen S. Wise was president of the Zionist Organization of America, he asked Morris Zeldin to become an organizational executive of the ZOA. Morris accepted with alacrity. The position with the ZOA gave Morris the opportunity to speak to congregations, Jewish centers, and Workmen's Circles all around the East Coast. His son Shy recalls that Morris was the most moving and engaging speaker in New York, especially in Yiddish, which was still widely spoken and understood. Morris was in great demand.

Unfortunately, due to pervasive Jewish and Zionist politics, Rabbi Wise was fired from his position as ZOA president. When he left, Morris also left. Fortunately for these two men, for Zionism and American Jewry, Wise was reinstated after a short period, and Morris returned to the ZOA. Morris was then integral in establishing the United Palestine Appeal, which later became the United Jewish Appeal. He was an inspiring and successful fundraiser.

Morris's personal and professional qualities were the soil that nourished his son Shy. Morris's love for and labor on behalf of the Jewish people, his teaching and speaking, and his organizational and fundraising skills were inherited by Shy and surpassed by him.

Some people have said that Morris was a tough guy. Shy could not be called tough. He was determined, never gave up, and was a visionary seeking to anchor dreams in reality by inspiring others. Thus, when Morris took Shy in 1933 to a rally protesting the rise of Hitler, he heard the powerful speeches of Rabbi Stephen

S. Wise and the Reverend John Haynes Holmes. Shy decided then and there to become a rabbi. He saw the rabbinate as the sure platform by which to defend the Jewish people. His father, Morris, was his model. Rabbi Stephen S. Wise was his ideal. Both men guided and mentored Shy.

After fifty years of service to the Zionist movement, a testimonial was held in Morris's honor. These are a few words that were spoken about him:

Morris A. Zeldin is one of a small handful of Zionist pioneers in America who have played a major role in bringing the message of Zion reborn to generations of American Jews. Active in the Zionist movement for more than fifty years, Morris Zeldin worked closely with major personalities of Zionist leadership, including the great Chaim Weizmann and Chaim Nachman Bialik. . ."

Morris was held in the highest esteem for his personal talents and passions for Zion and the Jewish people. His son Shy Zeldin imbibed Morris' lessons and built a rabbinate and a congregation that truly cast a giant beacon for Zionism, Jewish education, and social justice.

*Vision Looks Inward and Becomes Duty*

# 4

## The Early Years
### Envisioning Duty

SHY CONSIDERED HIS BIRTHDATE, July 11th, or 7/11, an omen of good luck. While it is not likely that Shy literally believed in luck, he did bring his many talents to create a successful personal and professional life. As a kid, he was close to his older brother, Jack, and to his younger brother, Bernie, who looked and sounded a lot like Shy.

The brothers could be rascals. There is a story about an odd practice in their shul. On Shabbat morning, men who were kohanim (claiming descent from the ancient Temple priests) removed their shoes outside the prayer room. Shy and his brothers used to sneak out and mix up the shoes. That fraternal closeness remained with them throughout their lives.

In his Brooklyn neighborhood, Shy was a leader among the local kids. His charismatic personality went hand in glove with his love of baseball and outstanding basketball skills. Later in his rabbinic career, Shy made it a practice to announce the World Series score when the High Holy Days coincided with the games. This was his own version of a seventh-inning stretch, and it kept the congregation in the auditorium.

Shy was also a disciplined golfer who enjoyed the camaraderie of the game. He excelled at chess. The ability to look ahead several moves would serve him well throughout his rabbinate.

Shy's parents, Esther and Morris, created a loving home. Morris was an autocrat who always encouraged his sons. Esther was a cultured and well-read person who spoke Yiddish, Hebrew, and English.

Shy was an outstanding student in the Talmud Torah and in high school. Following high school, Shy attended Brooklyn College. Even then, he was a visionary and an organizer. He became the president of the student Zionist society. He was committed to bringing Jewish studies onto the campus. Shy wanted Hebrew to be offered. The dean told him to find twenty-five interested students. Shy, in a preview of his future strength and determination, found twenty-five fellow students to enroll in Hebrew. Modern Hebrew became part of the curriculum of Brooklyn College.

Teaching and guiding kids was an early passion of Shy. In 1941, Shy took a job as a camp counselor. The camp was Hebrew-speaking. There, he met Florence Karp, who was a few months older than Shy. Flo, who had a degree in physical education, headed the sports program at camp. Her Hebrew name was Tsipporah. Shy tenderly called her Tsippi from before they married in 1943 and for the sixty-nine years of their marriage.

Florence came from a background similar to Shy. Her family was Orthodox, shul-going, and Jewishly literate. Florence and Shy welcomed their first child, Joel, to their family in 1947. Their second son, Michael, was born in 1950. Shy always credited Florence with shaping and guiding the character and quality of their family. Florence recognized that Shy was a hard worker and had great confidence in him. She always thought Shy knew what he was doing, and she said that Shy proved her right.

Florence partnered with Shy in his journey into the Reform rabbinate. They went to Cincinnati, where Shy enrolled in the Hebrew Union College. He viewed going to Cincinnati as a broadening experience that would take him west of the Hudson River. By the mid-1940s, HUC was no longer anti-Zionist.[1]

Shy's Hebrew and his knowledge of rabbinic texts were firmly implanted in him. As a result, the College recognized his acumen. Upon entering, out of a five-year program leading to ordination, he received credit for the first four years of the curriculum. During that year, Shy spent time tutoring classmates in Talmud. He served, as well, as a student rabbi on a bi-weekly schedule at a small congregation in Portsmouth, Ohio. In 1946, the College bestowed upon Shy rabbinic ordination as well as a Master of Arts in Hebrew Letters. The College also awarded him the Lazarus Prize for outstanding academic achievement. Thus, he crossed the threshold toward a brilliant future.

Upon ordination, the President of HUC, Dr. Julian Morgenstern, invited Shy to go to Stockton, California, to serve Temple Israel while its spiritual leader, Rabbi Levy, was away serving in World War II as an army chaplain. Shy then served as a civilian chaplain to military bases near Stockton, along with serving Temple Israel in Stockton. Eventually, Shy Zeldin would be known as an engaging, dynamic speaker, and Stephen S. Wise Temple, which he founded in 1964, would become the largest congregation on the West Coast with over three thousand families.

Temple Israel constructed a community center next door to the synagogue in 1925. Shy, in 1964, envisioned creating a community center at Stephen S. Wise Temple with a swimming pool, athletic fields, classrooms, and childcare facilities. He succeeded in making the temple a vibrant synagogue center.

After leading Temple Israel for a year, Shy moved to Congregation Bnai Jeshurun in Newark, New Jersey. He was the assistant rabbi there for two years. When Dr. Abe Franzblau, dean of the School of Education at HUC in New York, offered Shy the position of assistant dean, Shy readily accepted. Shy loved Dr. Franzblau and welcomed the opportunity to work with students. However, the salary he received was hardly adequate to support his family.

1. The Central Conference of American Rabbis voted to affirm and support Zionism in 1937. The UAHC took a pro-Zionist position in 1943.

He took a weekend pulpit at Temple Beth Sholom in Bayside Long Island to make ends meet.

Shy's best friend during his HUC days was Rabbi Jay Kaufman. Kaufman was the assistant to Rabbi Maurice Eisendrath, President of the Union of American Hebrew Congregations. At Eisendrath's bidding, Kaufman pressed Shy to go to Los Angeles to be the dean of the College of Jewish Studies. This was a tempting offer for Shy, who loved Jewish academics and teaching. The year was 1953, and institutions in the Jewish world were moving ahead in California. Further, Shy and Florence were no strangers to life in California since their time in Stockton. There were, however, some pitfalls to cope with.

Rabbi Kaufman also asked Shy to become the director of the regional office of the UAHC, whose purpose was to give support to congregational programs and administration. Shy, in essence, would be wearing two mantles of responsibility for two intense positions. To add to the stress, Rabbi Eisendrath urged Hebrew Union College president Dr. Nelson Glueck to make the College of Jewish Studies into the West Coast branch of the Hebrew Union College. Once HUC in Los Angeles came to fruition, Shy found himself serving two masters. There was no lack of tension between Glueck and Eisendrath, the giants of American Reform Judaism.

Shy was caught in the pincers of overbearing egos competing for the final say. Dr. Glueck was a world-renowned archaeologist and accomplished academic. Rabbi Eisendrath headed the UAHC, which funded a large percentage of the budget of HUC. Shy was hardly in a position to do more than take orders from polar opposites in the realm of leadership. Despite political challenges, Shy significantly increased the enrollment of the former College of Jewish Studies. Among its students was a substantial group that enrolled in the rabbinic program of the new West Coast Hebrew Union College led by Rabbi Zeldin. Some of the students who became rabbis were Lewis Barth, Sandy Ragins z"l, Allen Maller, Michael Signer z"l, Larry Goldmark, and Stephen Einstein.

A second pitfall, perhaps better thought of as a small pothole, was the strong objection of Joel Zeldin, Shy's eight-year-old son, to moving to Los Angeles. Joel did not want to be three thousand miles away from his beloved Brooklyn Dodgers. Shy managed to reassure his bereft son by promising Joel that the Dodgers would move to L.A. in three years. In fact, the Dodgers came to smoggy L.A. just before the start of the 1958 season. Joel was mollified by the promise and excited that "dem Bums" would come along to southern California.

How did Shy dare to make such a seemingly rash promise to Joel, a promise beyond his control? Joel has posited that Shy had a reliable inside source, a congregant who was "in the know." Joel suggests that Shy's source may have been Dory Schary, the screenwriter and well-connected producer-director who was probably a confidante of team owner Walter O'Malley. There may well have been an admirer of Shy from his congregation whose name is lost to us, who was another source. All we can say now is "TEYKU," the Hebrew acronym for Tishbi Y'tareitz Kushiot Uva'ayot—Elijah will solve all questions and conundra (when the Messiah arrives).

While Shy put Joel's Dodgers issue to rest, he could not tolerate the two positions he held with their two strong leaders. A slightly older colleague of Shy, Rabbi Bernard Harrison, had been the spiritual leader of Temple Emanuel of Beverly Hills. On the eve of Yom Kippur, 1957, Barney, as he was lovingly called, suffered a massive coronary. He died a few days later, leaving his community in deep mourning. Rabbi Harrison was a warm and caring person who connected with people. He was an inspiring speaker. He was not above rolling up his sleeves to grill hot dogs at the Purim carnival or to help decorate the Sukkah. Losing Barney so early in his life, at age forty-seven, was nothing less than a tragedy for Temple Emanuel. His absence, however, did create an opportunity for Rabbi Zeldin to move back into congregational life.

In 1957–58, Professor Marshall Sklar undertook a study of Jews in suburbia. This is a summary of his research. After World War II, Jewish religious observance declined, but there was greater pride in Jewish identity. Reform Jews were becoming somewhat more traditional as they felt increasingly at home in the suburban USA. Despite less observance, Jews were joining synagogues.

People wanted their children to have a Jewish education. Israel and Jewish causes gained wider Jewish support. The suburban synagogue became the predominant institution of Jewish life despite shrinking attendance at services.

The growth of synagogues created a window of opportunity for rabbis. Shy was known in the southern California area. His warmth, charisma, and brilliance made him an ideal candidate to follow Rabbi Harrison at Temple Emanuel. Rabbi Harrison had led Temple Emanuel to build a new synagogue in 1954 at a property it owned on Clark Drive. The facility included a sanctuary and chapel, a social hall, and school and youth facilities. Shy would eventually follow in the footsteps of synagogue-building rabbis by the decade of the '60s, 70s, and beyond. That would happen after Shy left Emanuel in 1964.

The board of Emanuel needed a rabbi to conduct Rabbi Harrison's funeral. They did not want to have a local congregational rabbi for fear that a charismatic person would attract away Emanuel's membership. Shy was recommended to the Emanuel board by the Union of American Hebrew Congregations, Reform Judaism's parent body in New York. Shy, at that time, was Dean of the Hebrew Union College in Los Angeles. The Emanuel leaders invited him to conduct the Harrison funeral. Ironically, they offered him the interim pulpit position. Shy accepted the pulpit of Temple Emanuel in 1958. The congregation was prestigious, and the facility built by synagogue architect Sydney Eisenstadt was modern yet warm and conducive to maintaining the community. What Shy did not know at first and what only became clearer as time went by was that Temple Emanuel was ruled by a group of oligarchs known as "The Big Board."

The board and its officers ran the show at Emanuel. They micromanaged Shy and were petty and critical. After Shy gave a sermon supporting a state ballot initiative to provide housing for the poor, some congregants complained it was too political. The board called Shy on the carpet and told him they wanted to see copies of his sermons in advance of his preaching them. Shy declined on two grounds. First, he refused to be censored. Second, he told the board he did not write sermons but gave them based on a brief mental outline. He said he had nothing to give them. He further told his inquisitors that he believed he was not talking politics but was applying Jewish ethics regarding care for the poor.

In addition to the board, which did not have a culture of respect or trust for the rabbi, Emanuel had an Executive Director who did not cooperate with Shy. He believed his authority was above that of the rabbi. Shy used to say that the E.D. wanted an accounting for every paper clip he used.

Shy found himself again in another vise. He was caught between a disrespectful board and an autocratic Executive Director. Shy continued for five years, putting up with humiliation and swallowing his bile. When the board accused him of surreptitiously interviewing for other jobs, Shy did indeed decide to resign as senior rabbi of Temple Emanuel. He told his wife and chief supporter, Tsippi, "I'd rather sell women's shoes than work at Temple Emanuel."

He sold not a single pair of sling pumps, but he did go on to create the largest, most dynamic shul in the U.S., Stephen S. Wise Temple.

*Vision Looks Outward and Becomes Aspiration*

# 5

## Stephen S. Wise Temple
### Becoming Aspiration

WHEN FAMOUS PEOPLE CAME to address the Stephen S. Wise Speaker's Forum, Shy always had his photo taken with the guest. Shy posed for a photo with the Dalai Lama. When the photo was developed, Shy had his secretary take it to be framed. She asked the frame store owner, "Do you know who that is in the photo?" The owner answered, "Well, I know the man on the right is Rabbi Zeldin, but I have no idea who the other guy is." Whether this story is based on an old joke in a new wrapping or actually happened is unknown. True or not, it conveys the degree of Shy's fame and reputation in southern California.

Shy's status in the Los Angeles basin grew with his conception and development of Stephen S. Wise Temple.

He had, as will be seen, a tremendous aspiration to create a unique synagogue center. His goal was to attract and involve as many Jews as possible to his congregation. His lifelong question and concern with regard to new practices and program initiatives was *Whether it was good for the Jews and Judaism*. If the answer was yes, he would say, "*Let's do it!*" Shy had two role models who influenced his direction and his rabbinic style. Rabbi Stephen S.

Wise, for whom Shy's father worked in the Zionist movement, conveyed strength, purpose, dignity, and wit. Once, Wise came late to a meeting of rabbis. The chairman pro tem invited Rabbi Wise to take his seat at the head of the table. Rabbi Wise demurred and took a seat on the side, saying, "Wherever I sit is the head of the table." Shy had greater modesty, but he appreciated Wise's frankness.

In the 1890s, Stephen S. Wise was the rabbi of Temple Beth Israel in Portland, Oregon. Congregation Emanu-El of the city of New York invited Wise to become their rabbi. Wise was about to accept the position when he received word that he would be required to submit his sermons in advance to the president of the congregation, Louis Marshall. That was too much for Wise. He declined Emanu-El's offer via telegram, which read, "I shall not submit to Marshall law!" This story made a deep impression on Shy, who always affirmed freedom of the pulpit for the rabbi.

Rabbi Mordecai Kaplan was the second major influence of Shy's rabbinate. Kaplan was originally ordained a Conservative rabbi but ultimately founded a new Jewish movement: Reconstructionist Judaism. He set out its principles in his book *Judaism As A Civilization* (1934). The essence of his view is that Judaism is not just a religion. It is an entire community embracing Jewish religion and peoplehood, culture, Hebrew language, and, ultimately, support for Israel. He advocated the observance of customs and rituals as the folkways of the Jewish people. The synagogue must be more than a place of worship. It must be a place where Jews meet, share Jewish culture, and grow strong. In short, all Jewish culture must be reconstructed to meet the needs of Jewish individuals and of the Jewish community. Shy was touched by Kaplan's vision. It became his aspiration to create Stephen S. Wise Temple.

When Shy and Temple Emanuel agreed to part, his buy-out contract stipulated that he would not start a new congregation within five miles of Emanuel. As he looked for a place where he might start a synagogue, he thought St. Alban's Episcopal Church would be an excellent locale, as it was on the cusp of Westwood and Bel Air. The minister, Reverend R. Parker Jones, warmly welcomed Shy and his yet to exist congregation. Shy went back to the Emanuel board to ask that they revise his exit contract to change the five-mile stipulation to 4.7 miles, the distance from Emanuel to St. Alban's on the eastern boundary of U.C.L.A. The Emanuel leaders thought he was joking and readily agreed to the revision he requested. And so it was that Shy led his first Friday evening Shabbat service at St. Alban's church in April of 1964.

Thirty-five founding families met with Shy to formally inaugurate the new congregation. One hundred eighty families left Emanuel, though not all of them joined Shy's congregation right away. Shy wanted to call his congregation The Free Synagogue in memory of his mentor Stephen S. Wise's fight for freedom of the pulpit. Among the founding members, some said that calling the congregation The Free Synagogue might lead some people to think that there would be no membership dues, an impossible situation. Shy had talked to his supporters about the leadership and devotion of Stephen S. Wise to the Jewish people and to Israel. Thus, it was hardly surprising that someone suggested the new congregation be called Stephen S. Wise Temple. Shy was of the opinion, influenced by Mordecai Kaplan, that anything that brings Jews together aligns with the purpose of the new congregation.

During the first three years, Stephen S. Wise Temple held Friday evening services at St. Alban's church in Westwood. Its minister, Rev. Parker Jones, enthusiastically supported Shy and his congregation. Rev. Parker Jones, on his own initiative, asked his custodian to cover the cross on Fridays, which hung over the pulpit. In addition to the Reverend's exquisite sensitivity, St. Alban's charged the Stephen S. Wise congregation no rent. Shy did insist on paying custodial fees.

Each Friday evening, the church sanctuary was completely full. Jews and non-Jews attended worship to hear Shy's stimulating sermons and to enjoy the music of Sheldon Marshall or Harvey Block. Shy had a custom-made Ark on wheels, which was stored in the back church closet. The Ark was painted gold with a seven-branched menorah carved on its doors with handles on its sides. It was exciting for those who came early to the church to remove the Ark from storage and take it up to the pulpit. There was an exhilarating sense of being pioneers on the threshold of creating a new Jewish congregation with a fresh communal outlook.

By mid-1964, one hundred eighty-five families comprised Stephen S. Wise Temple. That fall, under the visionary leadership of real estate developer Norman Feintech, the congregation purchased ten acres at Mulholland Drive and the San Diego Freeway. The location was ideal as the focal point between West Los Angeles communities and those of the San Fernando Valley. The first building was completed in 1968, which included classrooms as well as Hershenson Hall, a multi-purpose facility. It should be noted that the first wedding to take place in Hershenson Hall was that of Shy's elder son, Joel, to Karen Dash. In addition to being the main donor to build Hershenson Hall, Abe and Sylvia Hershenson donated office space in Beverly Hills to the congregation.

As the building process proceeded, the congregation grew. The board[1] originally voted to limit membership to 250 family units. They envisioned a small community of people dedicated to worship and study. When the congregation reached 250 families, the board, at Shy's urging, extended the membership to 250 families, then, in time, to 500, to 600, and to 1000. Shy persuaded the board to open the membership without limit. His position was rooted in his view that room must be made for any Jew wishing to identify and participate. He thought even atheists should belong to a synagogue community to be with fellow Jews. Shy intended Stephen S. Wise Temple to be inclusive and welcoming.

From the time of the building of Hershenson Hall, Stephen S. Wise Temple added a new building about every other year. The architect for the facilities was Larry Robbins. Shy would say of Larry that he built expeditiously, economically, wisely, and beautifully. At the dedication of the Westwood Sanctuary in 1970, City Councilman Zev Yaroslovsky remarked, "Well, Rabbi Zeldin, another year, another building permit!"

---

1. Shy used to say that a board is a long narrow object that seldom comes to a point. He would quote Dr. Nelson Glueck who said the purpose of a board is to hire a worthy rabbi, support or fire him, and otherwise to stay out of his way.

One may well ask how a growing congregation could afford to take on ever-increasing building projects. There are several answers. The first is Shy's extraordinary ability to raise funds and persuade people to participate. Shy could paint word pictures about programs, the needs of people, and the buildings to house them. Shy not only solicited people to give to various projects, but he made them feel grand about giving. When he looked back over his fundraising, he said he learned two important lessons: take the potential donor to lunch and solicit the gift at the end of lunch when the person feels full and relaxed.

There is a sweet story about a dentist whom Shy solicited from time to time. Shy called his office one day. The receptionist said the dentist was with a patient. Shy said his call would only take a minute. In a short while, the dentist came on the line. "Rabbi, I'm with a patient." Shy said, "I won't keep you long. Shimon, I just need twenty thousand dollars from you for our new parking structure." The dentist said, "Of course, I'll give it to you, Rabbi, but tell me why when you want money from me, you always call me by my Hebrew name." Shy replied, "Because when I do, you always respond positively, Shimon. Thank you."

Not everyone was capable of what Shimon the dentist did, but there was broad-based giving at different levels. All gifts were received with gratitude and encouragement toward the future. The fact that Shy always reached out to people in times of joy, need, or sorrow cultivated a desire in members to participate in the building projects and other fundraising efforts.

A major source of funds for the building of the Sanctuary, chapel, and offices was the congregation's merger with Westwood Temple in 1970 during the presidency of Sydney Dunitz. Westwood Temple was a small congregation on Santa Monica Boulevard. The leadership of Westwood Temple learned that the state of California and the city of Los Angeles would soon build a commuter line along that boulevard. The Westwood Temple leaders understood the congregation's days were numbered in that location. They approached Stephen S. Wise to propose a merger. Westwood Temple would turn over its assets to Stephen S. Wise Temple. In return, members of Westwood Temple would be able to continue their dues structure, which was less than that of Stephen S. Wise, for three years. Some of their board members would go on the Stephen S. Wise board. With the proceeds from the sale of Westwood Temple, Stephen S. Wise would build its formal Sanctuary to be called the Westwood Sanctuary in honor of their new partners. In addition to funds, Westwood Temple provided some of the outstanding leadership of Stephen S. Wise Temple, including Les Surlow, who became the congregation's president and supervised several of its building projects. Tillie Cytron is also remembered as a devoted and active leader who created a Wise Years group for seniors.

There were, along the way, substantial lay leaders of Stephen S. Wise Temple. For the most part, they were supportive of Shy. On the other hand, there was an incident when a lay leader publicly criticized Shy. After the meeting, Shy quietly took him aside. The rabbi told him he may criticize and complain all he wishes in private but not to contradict him in public. That little chat seemed to solve the problem and solidify Shy's leadership. One lay leader suggested years later that Shy was thin-skinned and insecure. An editor of one of the Los Angeles Jewish newspapers also levied the thin-skin charge against Shy. Other than this opinion, a similar view of Shy was never expressed by anyone else in research for this book.

The fact is that Shy knew well what he stood for and did not hesitate to engage those who opposed his support of Israel and the Jewish people's wellbeing.

Lay leaders understood Shy's reservoir of talents. He was a successful fundraiser. He could convey his vision to others. He could look ahead and see the moves that should be made to advance the goals he had for the Temple. He had an instinct for business. Someone once acknowledged his business acumen and asked him if he had the chance to be the CEO of a large company, would he do so? Shy replied, "No, I would still want to be a rabbi."

The core of his love for the rabbinate was the Jewish people and Jewish education. He thought anyone who wants a high-quality

Jewish education should get it. The synagogue school should be accessible to all, and everyone should be welcome. Shy saw to raise funds for the school to give scholarships to whoever needed help with tuition. Shy's philosophy was that the synagogue was not a country club. It needs to accommodate everyone. During an interview with Shy in 2016, former Stephen S. Wise Temple president asked Shy what he regretted about the high school he built. Shy answered that he wished he had created a special track for less academically oriented students who wanted a good Jewish education and Jewish community.

Shy was an innovator, and he was open to innovators on his staff. He encouraged the Parenting Center. He saw the value of starting a preschool to bring into the congregation young parents and to give children a foundation in the Jewish community. The preschool kids loved Shy and were drawn to him. The preschool became the impetus for starting a Day School, beginning with a first-grade class. Another class was added each year through grade six. The Junior High opened with the seventh grade. Eighth and ninth grades followed in consecutive years.

Shy's ultimate aspiration for the Stephen S. Wise Day School was to create a high school. The Conservative movement in Los Angeles had a high school called the Einstein Academy. It had serious financial trouble and, at mid-year, was about to close. This meant, in addition to the tragedy of losing a Jewish school, that the teachers would lose their salaries in the middle of the year. Shy, together with Michael Milken, raised the money to save the school. The teachers completed the school year with their salaries intact and their students in class. Einstein had to be disbanded at the end of the school year. Stephen S. Wise Temple assumed Einstein's debts. Michael Milken, at first, gave fifty thousand dollars to the school. Eventually, he contributed fifteen million dollars to the Stephen S. Wise High School.

It was fortuitous that Shy made the acquaintance of Abe Shpiegel, president of an Orthodox congregation. When Shy's friends Norman and Evelyn Feintech and Nathan and Lilly Shapell went to Hawaii with Shy and Florence, they introduced Shy to Abe

Shpiegel and his wife. It was Pesach, and Shy arranged to hold a seder. Grandchildren were also present. Shpiegel was so impressed with Shy's grandchildren's Hebrew skills acquired at the Stephen S. Wise Day School that he made a gift of one million dollars to the High School.

Shy took on the Milken High School project, despite its debt, in 1990 at the age of seventy. It was opened with one hundred fifty students. Shy's aspiration was lofty, and his task was gargantuan. At its zenith, the Milken School had more than eight hundred students. To help the school flourish, Shy made three important decisions. The first was to tell parents of students who belonged to other congregations to remain members of their own synagogues. Second, when parents who were members of other synagogues balked at donating to the Stephen S. Wise Temple Building Fund, Shy agreed to allow the school to withdraw from the congregation to exist independently as the Milken Community High School. A very proud and ethical decision Shy made was to place in the school's budget a five percent pension for teachers.

Though Milken Community High School in 2012 split off from Stephen S. Wise by mutual agreement, Shy had achieved his greatest of aspirations. He knew that the school he built would continue to educate students to the highest quality in an open, liberal Jewish educational setting.

Shy's granddaughter, Professor Sivan Zakai, says that her Grandpa Shy's greatest influence on her was the creation of the Day School. She loved the emphasis on Hebrew in the curriculum, along with learning the Bible and Midrash. Shy always said that his greatest fulfillment came from witnessing his grandchildren absorbing his and Florence's Jewish values. The education Shy's grandchildren received in the flourishing school validated all of Shy's efforts and aspirations.

The question might be asked: How could Shy, beyond retirement age, manage to establish the Milken High School? His answers included giving generous credit to his professional staff. He claimed it was because of the support and competence of his synagogue staff that he was able to focus on fundraising and developing the Milken High School. Shy never failed to acknowledge them publicly and with enthusiasm.

Shy's main partner in developing Jewish education and the Day School at Stephen S. Wise Temple was Metuka Benjamin. Shortly after the formation of the congregation, Shy reached out to Metuka to lead its educational program. Metuka had been on the faculty of Temple Emanuel. She was a "natural" as a teacher and a graduate of Columbia's Teacher's College. She gladly went to work with Shy. He was awed by her teaching skills and by her ability to kindle enthusiasm in her students through her positive energy. Her own leadership abilities resulted in Metuka's hiring top-quality and experienced teachers. She was a creative genius, an inspiring, caring educator, and an administrator par excellence. Metuka revered Shy for his warmth, people skills, and all-around brilliance. Their partnership was an ideal match with outstanding educational results for Stephen S. Wise Temple. Together, they were committed to providing a high-quality Jewish education to whoever wished it for their children. Shy and Metuka saw to giving scholarships and welcoming all students in a school accessible to all.

Rabbi Eli Herscher joined the Stephen S. Wise staff in 1975. He spent most of his rabbinic career with Shy, who was a guide, a mentor, and a colleague. Shy permitted Eli and other staff members a wide range of creative freedom. He felt mistakes were not the end of the world. One always learns and grows from one's errors. Shy's attitude toward "screw-ups" was "We can always fix it."

Eli became senior rabbi of Stephen S. Wise Temple in 1990. Shy told him, "You're now the senior. You can tell me what to do." Eli replied, "I will never tell you what to do." Eli was greatly beloved by many congregants for his sensitivity and ability to listen. Often, he was asked to officiate at member's life cycle occasions. Shy encouraged Eli and never resented that Eli was asked. Over the years, Eli grew from Shy's example. Shy always said, "When you do something for good, do it publicly so others may learn from it."[2] Rabbi Herscher certainly learned from Rabbi Zeldin, and Shy

2. In the realm of setting a public example, Shy used to pick up litter on the

appreciated Eli's admiration and support. Another addition to the staff was Cantor Nate Lam, who joined Stephen S. Wise's staff in 1976. An active temple member, Ed Sarnoff, heard the cantor at a performance and was bowled over. He called Shy and pressed him to look into hiring Nate. Shy interviewed Nate and offered the cantor's position to him that very day. He told Nate, "You're in charge of Services." Shy was thrilled with Nate. He once said to Nate with tears in his eyes, "If my father were alive, he'd be so pleased to see I finally have a chazzan with a traditional style." Indeed, Nate came from a traditional background, as did Shy. He really knew his stuff. So much was this the case that once, a young assistant rabbi asked Shy if he could create a service with a social justice theme. Shy said, "Sure, but go and see Nate about it. He's forgotten more liturgy than any of us will ever know." Cantor Lam contributed a variety of musical styles and programs for adults and youth, which fit Shy's vision of creating meaningful Services for modern, sophisticated Jews. Shy, Eli, and Nate were a dynamic team on and off the bimah.

In 1995, on the occasion of Shy's seventy-fifth birthday, Cantor Lam interviewed Rabbi Zeldin. He asked Shy what were his chief joys. Shy listed three areas: Family, Congregation, and Staff relations. What follows are stories that illustrate his lifelong commitment to finding and giving joy.

---

Temple premises, not leaving it to custodians and congregants.

# 6

## Shy's Chief Joys
### Aspirations for Family, Staff, and Congregation

WHEN THE ZELDINS MOVED to California in 1953, Shy, Florence, and sons Joel and Michael lived in a modest ranch-style home in Sherman Oaks in the San Fernando Valley. After Shy was engaged as the senior rabbi of Temple Emanuel, the Zeldins moved to a more spacious and welcoming home in Benedict Canyon. Shy was not into acquisitiveness or displays of materialism. He and Florence did wish, however, to enroll their sons in an outstanding school system. Technically, Zeldin's address was not in Beverly Hills, but being on the boundary line, Joel and Michael were enrolled in that school district known for its quality education.

Here are some memories of the Zeldin home and family, some of which I experienced personally. In the den or TV room outside the kitchen, the Zeldins had a small round table with a mosaic top made by a loving congregant. The mosaic pictured the key ceremonial objects for Havdalah, the Service that concludes Shabbat. Inlaid in the mosaic was a Kiddish cup, a spice box, and a multi-wick braided candle aflame. The colors of the tile were warm. They pulled you into the images in the table. They bespoke the depth of the Zeldins' caring for people expressed through their love of and devotion to Jewish ritual practice.

Beyond the den and kitchen was the dining room where the Zeldins would have Shabbat dinner or entertain guests. It was Shy's practice at dinner to raise a question or topic for discussion. He might bring up an ethical or political issue. He would often broach a Jewish contemporary topic or even a matter related to the goings-on at Stephen S. Wise Temple. Knowing that such was frequently their practice, as a dinner guest, I decided to raise a question. I asked why Rabbi Zeldin was creating new prayer liturgies and prayer books. His response was that contemporary Jews cannot relate to the old Union Prayer Book, last revised in 1940. I pursued the argument that it is up to rabbis, cantors, and teachers to lead the worshippers to understand the structure, themes, and aesthetics of the Reform Jewish Prayer Book with which I grew up. Shy waved away my point, saying we need to use our energies for new goals, such as bringing young Jews into the Temple. That requires new forms of prayer. Shy's son, Joel, has credited discussion and debate around their table as an exercise that helped prepare him for law school.

On the other side of the den were the bedrooms as well as Shy's and Florence's study. Let us take note of Joel's bedroom not for its unlikely neatness but for Joel's absence from it while he was at school at UC Santa Barbara. His bedroom became a refuge for a young man by the name of Ian Russ. Ian had been driving his family one night on Sepulveda Boulevard, a road that makes the Indianapolis Motor Speedway seem tame. When a drunk driver crossed the double line and hit them head-on. Ian's mother was killed. His father and brothers sustained serious injuries. Ian's face was shattered. He required multiple surgeries and rehabilitation. By the time many months went by, Ian sought to escape his trauma and despair. He told his best friend, Michael Zeldin, that he was about to depart for Europe to try to renew his spirit. When Ian went to say goodbye to Shy and Florence, Shy and Florence told Ian that they had been discussing his situation and thought it would help Ian to heal emotionally if he would live with them for a while. They assigned him Joel's room. Ian stayed for nearly a year, finding a wellspring of comfort, empathy, and support from Shy and Florence.

In later years, Ian wrote, "When I turned eighteen, Shy asked me to get a commercial driver's license so I could drive a school bus to bring kids to Day School. This showed me that despite the accident (not my fault), Shy trusted me. That contributed to my healing." According to Ian, Shy was not only his teacher and inspiration but the most significant male role model in his life besides his father.

Shy and Florence had a spacious, rectangular backyard. It could accompany 75–100 people easily. I was married by Shy there in 1968. A classmate of mine was also married there the same afternoon. My family provided the champagne glasses for the other family, who let us use their floral Chuppah. Shy's yard became a venue for the expression of love and community sharing.

The study in the Zeldin home was lined with floor-to-ceiling bookshelves. Many of Shy's books on Judaic subjects were collector's items of which he was quite proud. He used to show us Confirmation students around, pointing out various bound treasures he had gathered over the years. These tours made us aware of the depths of Jewish knowledge—a veritable sea— exciting for us to sample and, he hoped, to study. Such guided tours of Shy's study imprinted upon us the imperative to learn Torah.

Shy was truly a family man who worked assiduously with Florence to make their home a bastion of warmth and Judaic values. As is the case with many congregational rabbis, the demands on his time by the community could be like a tidal wave. Sometimes, personal needs and commitments had to be swept aside. Shy tried intensely to be home and present as much as possible. He was, as well, of the opinion that Florence was the linchpin holding their family together.

Michael, Shy's younger son, used to buy games to give Shy for his birthday. This was Michael's way to get Shy's time and attention since Shy liked games and enjoyed the precious engagement and the competition with his son. On the other hand, some of Shy's grandchildren complained that when they went out to a restaurant with Grandpa Shy, too many people would come to the table to talk to him, thus taking his attention from them.

Elder son Joel recollects that their home was a place where his parents transmitted not only love but clear values as well. They did this by setting standards and by being examples. Shy and Florence had strict expectations that their sons would maintain Kashrut, the Jewish dietary rules of Judaism. The boys were not permitted to plan social activities on Friday night, the eve of the Sabbath.

Joel and Michael learned life-shaping values from Florence and Shy. They learned to think for themselves and not to follow the crowd. If they wished to buy or do something because "everyone else is doing it," Shy would withhold permission. Shy's sons also observed that Shy would engage others to talk about their interests. He worked hard and played hard. He was not materialistic and wanted his sons to be people of ethical and spiritual substance. Both sons agree that Shy was a magnificent role model for ethical living. He never took advantage of people. He was helpful to friends and acquaintances. He never took monetary gifts.

Shy and Florence were generous to their children. They took their children and grandchildren on family trips to Israel, to Alaska, to the Caribbean. They wanted the cousins to know each other. They were ready to help as much as they could. When they sold their home, they gave each child a gift. They believed that whatever they had, they would share with their children. Shy always said, "Family is family. Help as much as you can. It doesn't diminish you; it adds to you."

Shy wanted his staff- professional, administrative, and custodial- to be a family as well. His daughter-in-law, Rabbi Leah Kroll, also a rabbi on staff, reveled in the sense of family at Stephen S. Wise. Shy engendered family feelings by reaching out, talking to staff, and showing interest in their lives. Once a staff member proved himself to Shy with hard work, follow through, and creative thinking, he said "yes" to most ideas and proposals. He was very warm and available. Leah remembers that Shy was magical with babies. He would sing a *niggun* (a Hassidic melody without words) to calm a crying baby. Actually, Shy could not carry a tune. Possibly, the infants stopped wailing to quiet Shy's gravelly voice!

Rabbi David Woznica, the Director of the Center for Jewish Life at the congregation since 2004, had an affectionate relationship with Shy. He noted that Shy interacted with people and always had time for individuals. Shy had patience for people and was calm and confident. He welcomed all who came to the synagogue. In short, Rabbi Woznica claimed that Shy gave everyone "the million-dollar treatment." He felt Shy was a supportive father figure.

Raz Husayni, Media and Production Manager, has been on the staff of Stephen S. Wise Temple for thirty years. He provided substantial guidance for me while researching this biography through the Temple archives. When he shared with me his feelings about the connection to Stephen S. Wise Temple, I knew his sentiments spoke for scores of people on staff. Raz told me, "Stephen S. Wise is not my workplace, but my family. It is not my job but an extension of my life. That aura which Shy created is still over the Temple community."

Former Governor of California Gray Davis has been a member of Stephen S. Wise Temple since 1995. He is also a faithful, church-going Catholic. He admired Shy and his principles. Shy, in turn, honored Governor Davis by giving him a seat on the bimah during the High Holy Days. Governor Davis recalls that Shy held to four principles both in his life and in the building of the Temple. Those principles were abbreviated by an acronym that Shy created: L.I.F.E.

L = Loyalty;
Shy believed in loyalty to staff and toward members with an expectation of reciprocity.

I = Israel.
We will focus on Israel later.

F = Flexibility.
Shy believed the congregation must be flexible in liturgy and music, in welcoming mixed married families, and in meeting life needs, whether for the elderly or young parents.

E = Enthusiasm.
Shy said publicly, "Whatever we do, we do with enthusiasm." To that end, he frequently quoted the Book of Ecclesiastes: "Whatever your hand finds to do, do with all your might." In other words, live with gusto; put energy into what you do.

Shy was a great role model for the first letter of the acronym, L, for loyalty. He stood by Governor Davis when he was recalled from office, an effort led by radical right-wing organizers. Shy did his part to overcome the Governor's public humiliation by continuing to invite the Governor to sit on the bimah during High Holy Days. The Governor, with his wife Sharon, returned the loyalty by accompanying Shy and Florence to get ice cream after Services. The Governor did not eat ice cream at night before bed but stood with Shy as he indulged his joy with a sundae.

Likewise, when businessman and philanthropist Michael Milken was indicted and convicted of participating in a junk bond scheme, Shy stood up for him and was supportive. Shy insisted on keeping the name of the Milken High School.

Even in the earlier days at Temple Emanuel, Shy gave respect and comfort to those who needed bolstering. His congregant, Dr. Abraham Abarbanel, an OB-GYN, was found guilty of performing an illegal abortion in 1962. The doctor was further accused of malpractice. The Court of Appeals ultimately reversed Dr. Abarbanel's conviction. The court did not find him guilty of performing an illegal abortion because he took the word of professional colleagues, both psychiatrists, that the patient's life would be in danger unless she terminated her pregnancy. With a clear statement of support, Shy honored Dr. Abarbanel with a seat on the bimah on Yom Kippur Eve despite the controversy in the congregation over the case.

Flexibility was Shy's third principle for a successful synagogue. Steven Fink, past president of the congregation, joined the Temple because of its flexibility at Services. Part of that flexibility in Fink's view was an ardent welcoming of children at the Temple. Indeed, Shy was practical and non-dogmatic when it came to liturgy, as Cantor Lam stated. As has been mentioned, Shy created liturgies and encouraged staff to do so as well. At the same time, Shy also recognized that the Reform movement was heading in a more traditional direction. Shy was open to Cantor Lam's teaching trope (Torah cantillation) to Day School students. Besides liturgy and worship, Shy's flexibility extended to establishing a wide variety of programs: the Parenting Center, Mommy & Me, Holiday Workshop, swimming, and sports programs, Wise Women, and many other adult education programs.

Enthusiasm was foundational to Shy's personal and professional life. Shy taught his grandchildren a lesson that guided his own life: "Learn to love what you have to do." This kind of attitude fills the activities of one's life with tremendous energy, focus, and success. (Incidentally, Shy ate broccoli every day because he thought it was healthful. He learned to love it, though it was not his favorite vegetable). The current senior rabbi of the Temple, Yoshi Zweiback, recalls that Shy had a great sense of service, enthusiasm, and passion for everything. Shy once told Rabbi Yoshi how he gets people to show up for events. He'd advise, "Go through the Rolodex (an old-fashioned telephone file) to invite people personally to attend a particular event or program." That takes a contagious, enthusiastic effort that always leads to substantial attendance. Aviva Feintech summed up Shy's approach, saying he provided the energy and commitment to the Congregation.

Shy's philosophy of L.I.F.E. was the impetus for him to create Stephen S. Wise Temple. He was committed to connecting Jews to Torah and Jewish learning, to community building through the synagogue, and through supporting Israel. He affirmed the idea that the Jewish future depends upon creating knowledgeable, community-oriented Jews. Education is the chief guarantor of Jewish existence. Not numbers alone, but a commitment to Jewish identity and values is the hope of a flourishing Jewish people.

*Vision Looks Upward and Becomes Faith*

# 7

## Faith of a Modern Rabbi

I CAN SAY UNEQUIVOCALLY that never, as a teen nor as an adult, have I heard a rabbi read the prayer book with the feeling and attention Shy brought to it. His voice was resonant, relaxed with warmth. When he blessed me on my Bar Mitzvah, I felt close to him, close to the congregation. He touched my soul. His faith transmitted itself to me in prayer as well as in his teachings and his activities.

As a doorway to explore Shy's faith in the coming chapters, we spend some brief time now on Jewish definitions of faith. The kind of so-called faith that is an unquestioning affirmation of a set of dogma is not the way of Jewish faith. The Hebrew word for faith is *Emunah*. One of the great Reform rabbis of the twentieth century and a Zionist leader was Abba Hillel Silver (1893–1963). He wrote, "*Emunah* in Judaism is not a creed or a belief. It is steadfastness to a course prescribed, firm and zealous adherence to a code of moral practice, and confidence in the right outcome of . . . all action willed by God" (according to Torah).[1]

Another mid-twentieth-century rabbi, Leo Baeck (1873–1956), was a survivor of the Nazi concentration camp at Theresienstadt. He taught, "In Judaism, faith is nothing but the living

1. Condensed from Silver, *Where Judaism Differed*, 174.

consciousness of the Omnipresent . . . It is the capacity of the soul to perceive the permanent in the transitory. Man's creative ability is manifested in his ability to do good. By experiencing the reality of the good, man is able to shape his own soul."[2]

Baeck and Silver's views on faith may be summed up simply. Faith is

1. Commitment to living a moral life

2. Confidence in the reality and ultimate victory of the good

3. Affirming our ability to shape our souls

In 1996, Shy wrote a book entitled *What This Modern Jew Believes*. He sets out his beliefs on key Jewish ideas. His material and presentation are quite accessible to the lay reader. This chapter will explore Shy's religious positions and his *Emunah*, both theoretical and activist. The following chapters will examine how Shy gave his faith "flesh and bones" through a variety of responses to issues and challenges in his life's work. The beauty of Shy's book is that Shy did not write it as a philosopher or theologian. It is straightforward. He admitted he was not a theologian but an eclectic thinker influenced by Mordecai Kaplan, Martin Buber, and Hassidic teachers. He described himself as following the rational philosophers rather than the proponents of Jewish mysticism.

As Kaplan taught, God is naturalistic, not anthropomorphic. This means that God is not human-like, not literally a controlling diving king. God is not a person or personality but rather the creative force in the universe that enables us if we are so committed, to see and to do the ethical good. When we pursue in our lives what is ethical, that is a moment of what Kaplan calls "salvation."

Shy was disappointed in many Jews who claimed to be agnostics or atheists. He understood their rejection of Biblical views of God. What he found difficult was their failure to study and to engage with adult, intellectually sophisticated views of God. This is a summary of Shy's beliefs:

---

2. Baeck, *Essence of Judaism*, 119. Gendered language not corrected.

1. God created the universe and allowed it to run according to the laws of nature.

2. God has built into the laws of nature a *moral spirit* so that good ultimately triumphs over evil.

Along with these points, Shy affirmed that we know God from what God does, just as Moses knows God as the source of liberation, morality, justice, and compassion.

Even though Shy and Kaplan rejected the notion of God as a person, they still saw purpose and value in prayer. Shy tells us he prays to God for strength and courage to do his life's work. Shy was faithful to the idea that God is his partner, but God cannot act without human participation.[3] He affirmed that if we want God in our lives, if we seek God, God becomes close to us. Prayer and communal Services, therefore, connect us to God, to Jewish values, and to our people.

Kaplan rejected the notion that the Jews or any other group were chosen by God. Shy did not reject the term or the concept. However, he understood it to define the purpose of the Jewish people in the world: to teach morality both through what we affirm and how we behave. The Jewish people should be a role model of ethical living. Whether we are consistent in our sacred task or stumble along the way, this ideal vocation in the world is the core of the Jewish Covenant with God.

The Covenant has been understood to mean that the Jewish people follows God's laws as sacred and timeless as presented in the Torah, and God guarantees the survival of the Jewish people. Shy interpreted the sacred and timeless element of Torah to be the ethical laws. For him, the Orthodox minutiae of ritual laws have been subject to change over the millennia and are not the essence of the Covenant. Yet Shy understood Jewish religious practice as binding together the Jewish people even as Kaplan saw Jewish ritual as the folkways of the people of Israel. For Shy, the origin of Jewish law is human insight and presentation. Likewise, centuries

3. Zeldin, *What This Modern Jews Believes,* 139–140, revised in the Stephen S. Wise High Holy Day Machzor.

of legal interpretation and expansion are man-made. Without turning to supernaturalism, Shy understood Jewish law to be the instrument for preserving the Jewish people.

It stands to reason that with Shy's affirmation of natural as opposed to supernatural religion, he neither believed in miracles nor in the coming of a saving messiah. He thought that making the idea of a messiah a prominent part of faith undermines efforts for self-fulfillment and group moral progress.

Shy's deepest commitment was his *Emunah* to cultivate the soul. He thought the primary purpose of our lives and our most challenging summons is to raise up the soul to its highest level. The soul is the spiritual and ethical force within each person. There is a soul in each one of us. Upon death, our souls return to God, their source. Our goal is to return our souls, so to speak, to a state as pure as we received them from birth. This soul cultivation rests upon our deeds of caring and compassion, our work for justice in the world, and our devotion to the Jewish people.

Two activities, in Shy's view, especially enable us to cultivate our souls. It is the path to absorbing Jewish values. Cultivation of the soul through Jewish education was the motivating energy for Shy's work as a visionary and fundraiser for the schools of Stephen S. Wise Temple. He believed that America is a symphony in which Jews must play their part by raising children and teens to be Jewishly literate. He was convinced that Jewish education at the high school level ultimately would determine whether there would be a viable future for liberal Jews. We need high schools, youth groups, camps, and Israeli learning experiences. Learning and prayer in a communal setting are the chief tools for soul cultivation.

Shy summarized the essence of his belief in these words quoted in the front of this biography:

"Your soul, that I don't know and that I cannot see, exists just as much as your physical attributes. That soul, your *neshama,* is what life is all about. The cultivation of each person's *neshamah* is essentially the challenge of human existence."[4]

---

4. Zeldin, *What This Modern Jew Believes,* 139–140, revised in the Stephen S. Wise High Holy Day machzor.

The following chapters illustrate how Shy acted and encouraged others to cultivate souls through social justice.

# 8

# Community Strengthens *Emunah*

SHY WAS ONCE AUDITED by the IRS. The tax people claimed he was improperly deducting the cost of his phone. Shy made a good case for that deduction. He told the IRS that he spends a great deal of time on the phone with Temple members. He pointed out that even asking someone on the phone how he/she is often elicits a litany of dilemmas, problems, or sadness. Much of Shy's counseling of people in need happened over the phone. The phone, therefore, is a deductible professional tool. The IRS backed down. Shy prevailed.

The IRS incident conveys more than merely standing up to the taxation folks. It tells how diligently Shy paid attention to individuals in the congregational community. A woman who had been a student of Shy's relied on him while she was going through a divorce. He gave her advice when she asked for moral support. She remembered he would call her from time to time to listen to her and to bolster her. Shy was available on a personal, caring basis to the Stephen S. Wise Temple members as well as to others in greater Los Angeles.

Shy was an extremely hard worker. He told Rabbi Eli Herscher, who was interviewing to join that staff that he worked twice as hard as other rabbis and expected hard work from his staff. Much of Shy's labor was directed toward the individual needs of congregants and to building community at Stephen S. Wise Temple.

Community and individual needs were the basis of a six-year debate in the congregation about membership size. The congregation was founded with thirty-five families who supported Shy. Many of them wanted to limit membership to two hundred and fifty families. They envisioned a relatively small community of people dedicated to worship and study. They may have been influenced by the Leo Baeck Temple, which had a limited membership and a reputation for Jewish intellectual pursuit, spiritual worship, and social justice. Reality did not reflect the ideal. People wanted to be part of the congregation. As more people knocked on the door at Stephen S. Wise, the Board, at Shy's prodding and insistence, kept revising its by-laws to expand the membership numbers. Between 1964 and 1969, the membership quota continued to be enlarged until it reached 1,450 members.

In 1970, Westwood Temple merged with Stephen S. Wise. Shy encouraged the Stephen S. Wise members to reach out to welcome the Westwood members. With the addition and absorption of the Westwood congregation, Shy called for an open membership policy. He explained to the congregation that the future of Jewish life in America is threatened. He pointed out that forty percent of Jews nationally are unaffiliated. Sixty percent of Jews west of the Rockies do not belong to a congregation.

Shy, therefore, thought it was unconscionable to keep out Jews who wished to belong. He felt that a limited congregation is "country club exclusive." He said, "I writhe trying to live with the concept."[1] He argued that the only legitimate reason for keeping people out is space limitations. He pointed out that the original development plan called for three more classrooms yet to be built but which could be easily added. He displayed his financial acumen by pointing out that large congregations can afford professional personnel and teachers. Whatever the cost of expanding membership, income from new members' dues more than covered it. He was very clear about his position, saying, "My life is dedicated

1. *Amarim* June 1969.

to making more and better Jews. The Stephen S. Wise Temple is our vehicle for doing just that."[2] So it was that, after six years of discussion and debate, the Board voted to open the membership of Stephen S. Wise to all who wished to be part of this Jewish community.

"Making more and better Jews" does not quite express the depth of Shy's *Emunah* for the community. On the eve of departing on a Sabbatical Caribbean cruise, Shy wrote in the Temple bulletin, "We look upon our life's task as serving our families . . . We relish our attachments to so many people and their attachments to us."[3] Upon ending the six-month Sabbatical, Shy said, "One thing we missed in all this time was our involvement with our community of Temple members. It led us to the conclusion that, for us at least, the need to be part of a larger family working for a greater cause was part of the excitement of living."[4]

Shy often said that anything that brings Jews together is aligned with the goals of Stephen S. Wise Temple. His philosophy of congregational life was whatever a group of individuals wanted the Temple to espouse, for personal enrichment or for community improvement, would be housed and nurtured by the congregation. This philosophy was foundational to making the Congregation an arena for innovation in programs as well as in areas of personal needs. Among the Stephen S. Wise innovative programs, we list the following:

- The Parenting Center
- Single Parents Support Group
- Singles in Transition
- Jewish Lamaze Group
- You and Your Aging Parent
- Grandparents Group

2. *Amarim* June 1969.
3. *Amarim* February 1973.
4. *Amarim* April 1973.

- PMS Support
- Stepmoms Support Group
- Step-parenting Support Group
- Parents of Disabled Children Support Group
- Support Group for the Newly Bereaved

In addition, under the guidance of Rabbi Eli Herscher in the late 1970s, thirty Havurot[5] were established.

Despite Shy's *Emunah* for the community, he never thought merely being a dues-paying member, a name on a membership roster was sufficient. His motto was you do have to be Jewish to be Jewish. By that, he really meant you have to *do* Jewish to be Jewish. He was of the opinion that in voluntaristic, individualistic America, there would be no Jewish future unless Jews practiced their faith and values. There needs to be greater Jewish self-acceptance and participation. Jewish families must observe Shabbat and holidays. People need to attend Shabbat Services with regularity, even if only for cultural and communal identification.[6] They ought to read Jewish books and periodicals and take adult classes. Thus, to be Jewish, you have to be conscious as an active celebrant. Community is the sacred arena for our Jewish identity. Following the Yom Kippur War of 1973, Shy reminded his congregation that while their devotion and monetary support of Israel was exemplary after the danger was past, we must go back to the details of Jewish life: prayer, study, and pursuing justice.

When the merger of Stephen S. Wise Temple and the Westwood Temple was complete, Shy wrote in *Amarim* a word of welcome. He summed up what his yardstick was for a successful congregation:

"A congregation is made up of people. People are individuals. In the final analysis, the worth of a congregation is measured by

5. A *Havurah* is a group of eight to twelve couples who meet regularly for study and discussion, socializing, or for cultural activities and for Jewish celebration. *Havurot* help root people in a smaller community within a large congregation.

6. *Amarim* April 1971.

the effect it has on the lives of individuals and how these lives are broadened and enriched. Further, any Temple that attracts people to an activity needs to bring them into the larger congregation."[7]

Shy did so by spending hours on the phone, reaching out to people, and inviting them to events and classes. His ears and his heart were open to all, with the exception, perhaps, of the IRS.

7. *Amarim* June 1970.

# 9

# Reform Do's and Dues

SHY'S ORTHODOX FATHER, MORRIS, it will be recalled, urged his son to apply to the Reform seminary, Hebrew Union College. Morris recognized that Shy was of an independent mind as well as a courageous soul. The Reform philosophy and setting fit Shy.

A foundational position of Reform Judaism is the conviction that the Bible is a human document, not a direct, divine revelation. Thus, unlike Orthodox Judaism, which sees the Bible as divine and rests the authority of Jewish law in God, Reform places authority for ritual observance in the individual and in the community. Shy used to teach that the rigid positions of Orthodox Judaism were not grounded in the Jewish reality of change throughout our history.

Shy pointed out that even the Bible, since the time of Moses, presented changes in Jewish law and practice. The Book of Numbers altered the law of inheritance and property. That law was expanded to include women as heirs if there were no male relatives.[1] Further, with the destruction of the second Temple, animal sacrifice was replaced by prayer, study, and loving deeds, which elevated the spiritual above the physical. Shy taught that traditional Judaism has been in a constant state of change since

---

1. See Numbers 27:1–11.

its earliest days. The bottom line for Shy was just as our ancestors altered Jewish practice to preserve the Jewish people; we may do so as needed in our day.

Shy advocated that two questions must be asked as guidelines for what practices we maintain, adapt, or adopt:

1. Is it good for the future of the Jewish people in the United States?

2. Is the proposed change in practice made with integrity and sincerity?

In the next chapter, we will examine how Shy applied his Reform principles to the issues around mixed marriage.

Reform Judaism was liberating for Shy. To him, it was not freedom from observance but a source of choice and deepening of commitment. He personally continued to maintain Kashrut but did not impose it on his Congregation. Yet Shy felt that American Reform Judaism had made a mistake in putting aside too much traditional practice. At Stephen S. Wise, all the Jewish holidays and festivals had a place for observance and celebration on the calendar. He encouraged Cantor Lam to bring more traditional music and more Hebrew into Services. Shy's devotion to Jewish learning as the source of Jewish survival was a deeply traditional value. Israel and Zionism were front and center in the synagogue community.

Shy's love of tradition did not inhibit his desire to innovate. He believed Judaism must speak to the needs of contemporary Jews. Leaders and rabbis have to be learned and wise. He encouraged writing new liturgies that infused Jewish values with fresh language and inspiring metaphors. The staff collaborated to create *The Stephen S. Wise Temple Machzor*. The goal was to be relevant, thought-provoking, and aesthetically touching. With the new prayers, Cantor Lam introduced new music. For Shabbat Sukkot, dance and pulpit drama were added as well. What Shy set out to accomplish was summed up in the words of Avraham Yitzchak Kook (Chief Rabbi of the Ashkenazi Palestine community 1929–1935): "The old shall be renewed, and the new shall be made holy."

Shy had a foot in his Orthodox past and a foot in the dynamism of Reform Judaism. He sometimes used the former to advance the latter.

For example, Cantor Lam was once requested to co-officiate with an Orthodox rabbi at a wedding. The Orthodox rabbi did not want to allow Cantor Lam to chant the *Sheva Brachot*, the Seven Wedding Blessings. The Orthodox rabbi claimed that because Cantor Lam was not a *Shomeir Shabbat*, a strict Sabbath observer, he may not fulfill his role of chanting the wedding blessings. Cantor Lam reported to Shy the Orthodox rabbi's refusal to allow him to participate. Shy offered to call the Orthodox rabbi, and Cantor Lam readily agreed. A while later, Shy called Cantor Lam to say it's all worked out. The Orthodox rabbi agreed that Cantor Lam would be the final authority on the liturgy. Apparently, Shy, with his Orthodox roots, knew how to get through to the Orthodox rabbi. He surely reminded him that Jewish law does not require the person who chants the Seven Blessings to be a strict Sabbath observer.

Shy loved the tradition, but as far as he was concerned, it had to make sense. Despite the traditional elements he brought to Services, he never tried to introduce the Musaf Service. *Musaf* means "additional service," which recalls and replaces the extra sacrifice Jews offered on Shabbat when the Temple in Jerusalem was still the focal point for sacrificial worship. Since Jews no longer worshiped through sacrifice, Musaf made no sense to Shy in a Reform Service even though it was still recited in Conservative and Orthodox synagogues. He would always apply common sense to the options before him. Shortly, we will see further such examples.

Shy's devotion to Reform Judaism did not prevent him from entering into a major confrontation with the parent body of the Movement, the Union of American Hebrew Congregations. The Union fulfilled several functions: supplying a substantial part of the budget for the Hebrew Union College; publishing textbooks for religious schools and for adult education; maintaining regional offices for support and programming in congregations; and providing a national voice for Reform values, especially in areas of social justice. Shy approved of the extensive work of the UAHC.

The reader may recall that in 1953, Shy accepted the position of director of the western regional office of the Union. Shy was clearly familiar with the work of Reform's national body. However, he did feel that Stephen S. Wise Temple, with its extensive programs, required little from the UAHC.

The break between Shy and Stephen S. Wise Temple from the UAHC came about over the Union's dues requirements for member congregations. In the early to mid-1990s, the Union insisted that congregations pay twelve percent of their operating budget to the national body. In real terms, Stephen S. Wise Temple owed the Union $200,000 in annual dues. Adding to the financial stress was a degree of recession in the California economy in the nineties. Shy was working day and night as well to raise funds for building the Milken High School, whose cost was twenty-five million dollars. What the Union required, in Shy's view, was simply too much of a fiscal burden. In negotiations with the Union for dues adjustment, Shy sought two elements. First, he and Stephen S. Wise Temple would agree to pay $100,000 a year for five years. The second idea Shy suggested was for the Union to levy dues on a per capita basis of the number of members of Congregations. He pointed out that national Protestant bodies assessed dues on a per capita basis. If the Union were to adopt a per capita dues system, he and his congregation would support it.

Shy was not a lone voice in the Reform Movement about the amount and structure of its dues policy. Two hundred congregations demanded change in the Union dues structure for relief in their budgets. Wilshire Boulevard Temple under Rabbi Edgar Magnin withdrew from the Union— a partial influence on Shy. Other rabbis in the Los Angeles community defended the Union and its dues requirements. Some pointed out that the budget of the UAHC was lean and responsible. They highlighted the Union's sustaining role in the Hebrew Union College. Rabbis declared their appreciation for the Union's stand on matters of social justice. There was a fear that disagreement over the dues requirements would lead to the balkanization of the Reform movement.

Shy and the leadership of Stephen S. Wise Temple were not able to persuade the leaders of the UAHC for dues relief. The result was the expulsion of the Congregation from the Union in 1995. In time, a compromise was reached. Stephen S. Wise rejoined the Union. Today, the Union for Reform Judaism has five different forms of dues structures so that each congregation can participate within its means. Shy, Stephen S. Wise, and many other leaders and congregations brought about an evolution toward equitable and accessible URJ dues. The URJ leadership was listening and, ultimately, receptive and fiscally creative. Shy, in the long run, continued to advocate the do's of Reform Judaism while making his peace with the dues of the national movement.

# 10

## Jewish Identity and Survival

On Wednesday afternoons, about sixty sixteen-year-olds would gather in the Chapel of Temple Emanuel for the Confirmation class with Rabbi Zeldin. He spoke to us on many topics, from sexual ethics to Israel and Bible and Jewish history. One topic I clearly remember about which Shy spoke to us kids as well as to the congregation from the bimah was mixed marriage. According to the rabbi, mixed marriage was exogamy, marrying a partner who is not Jewish nor is interested in conversion to Judaism. This is different from intermarriage, where the partner who is not Jewish converts to Judaism prior to the wedding. This circumstance is endogamy, or "marrying in," the result of which should be creating a Jewish home with Jewish children.

The rabbi spoke to us in the most definite and unhesitating terms about the negatives of mixed marriage. He told us that research shows that mixed marriages end up in divorce court four times more often than endogamous marriages. Mixed marriages, said the Rabbi, threaten the future of Judaism and the Jewish people. The preservation and strengthening of both were always Shy's foremost goals. Not only did Shy not approve of mixed marriage, he, of course, declined to officiate at them until 1970, the year he turned fifty.

We have written about Shy's flexibility in thought and deed. In 1970, he published an article in *Amarim*, the synagogue bulletin, "An Old Position on Mixed Marriage Re-examined— and Somewhat Modified." It is astounding that a rabbi, more than halfway through his career, would re-think and alter a principle he had maintained for twenty-five years. That he could change a long-held, values-based view of mixed marriage speaks volumes about his insight and his character.

Shy was well aware that the rate of mixed marriage between Jews and non-Jews was increasing in substantial numbers in the U.S. He knew that eighty percent of young Jews went to university. They met many people not of their religious or ethnic background. They dated outside their faith and cultural community. Shy realized that preaching against mixed marriage and refusing to officiate would not reduce or change the growing rates of mixed marriage. He determined that the question he and other rabbis now faced was how to keep the households and the children of mixed marriages firmly anchored in Judaism. In other words, while his tactics would change, his ultimate preservation goals for our people and our faith remained strong.

Shy, in rethinking his goals, did not open the floodgates to support mixed marrying couples unequivocally. He demanded a high degree of certainty that a mixed marrying couple was committed to building a Jewish home with Jewish observance. To assure himself, Shy conducted several interviews with the couple. He also wanted to know if the woman had had a Jewish education, at least through Confirmation. If she did not, he asked her and the partner, if possible, to enroll in an Introduction to Judaism class. Shy did not extend his officiating to couples where the husband was Jewish, but the wife was not. He felt the woman was the main shaper of religious tradition in the home, not the husband. A non-Jewish, unconverted mother would have difficulty in this. The Jewish father would be likely too busy outside the home to pick up the duties of education and Jewish calendar observance in the home. If there were a divorce and the children remained with their non-Jewish mother, there was a good chance of Judaism being erased from their lives. While there is no circumstance in which there will be a one hundred percent positive outcome for Jewish identity, Shy wished to do all he could to add another Jewish home full of Jewish children to the Jewish community. In sum, Shy reasoned, "The growing rate of mixed marriage in the U.S. and around the world need not result in losses to the Jewish community if we are wise enough to guide the Jewish mate to raise children as Jews."[1]

As a result of Shy publicly supporting mixed marriage, if the woman is Jewish, there was a sharply critical reaction to his position by the Orthodox community. Rabbi Maurice Lamm, a leader in the Orthodox community, had taken to task Reform Judaism and UAHC President Rabbi Alexander Schindler over the conversion issue. Lamm objected to Schindler's encouragement of the Reform community to seek converts to Judaism actively. Lamm accused this position of "shocking Reform Judaism to its roots."[2] He said Reform's stance bespoke an "ailing Reform movement." Shy offered a vigorous reply that not only was Reform Judaism not ailing, but it was the largest Jewish synagogue body in the U.S. and Canada, with over 733 congregations affiliated with it.

Shy answered Rabbi Lamm based on observations in his rabbinate. Shy stated, "My own experience indicates that where mixed married families are taken into Reform congregations, the family is more committed, more observant, and the children of those families better-motivated students than the average Jewish family where both parents were born Jewish."[3]

It is well known that Jewish law (developed by rabbis 200 B.C.E. - 600 C.E.) takes the position that a child follows the religious and ethnic identity of its mother. Lamm demanded that this matrilineal principle be upheld by all Jews. Shy argued that the criteria of Jewish law are often contrary to the realities of contemporary Jewish life. For example, there are cases where the child of a Jewish mother may have been circumcised but is sent to Christian Sunday School at the father's urging and is part of the church

1. *Amarim* March 1980.

2. *Amarim* February 1981.

3. *Amarim* February 1981.

community. Shy, despite the Jewish legal status of the mother and the circumcision, could not recognize the child as Jewish. His view was, essentially, we are what we experience. A child who experiences Christian teaching, Christian youth group, and church Services is likely to identify wholly as a Christian and not as a Jew.

Shy, himself of Orthodox background, goes on to explain his understanding of the difference between Orthodox and Reform Judaism. He tells us that Orthodoxy sees Halacha (rabbinic law) as synonymous with Judaism. "Reform seeks a pluralism which respects Orthodox decisions, but which will not determine the lives of its adherents. The Orthodox, unfortunately, cannot get themselves to understand Reform viewpoints even though they disagree."[4] Shy could envision what the Orthodox could not: a Jewish community of many families with a converted parent who came to Judaism because of Reform's open door.

Shy began rethinking his view on mixed marriage in the late 1960s and wrote his article quoted above in 1970. At this time, a majority of Reform rabbis were not officiating at mixed marriages. In fact, it was extremely difficult for mixed couples to find a rabbi to officiate at their wedding. I did not begin to officiate for mixed couples until seven years after my ordination. Some of our colleagues did not begin to officiate at mixed marriages until late into their rabbinic careers. One Rabbi, I recall, did not change his position until some forty years into his rabbinate. Indeed, reflection, evaluation, and change as needed are hallmarks of Reform Judaism.

It took the Reform movement as a whole another decade to develop its view on the identity of children in a mixed marriage. Shy reported on a meeting of rabbis in New York he attended to define the question of who is a Jew. The resolution they came up with was as follows:

> Where only one of the parents is Jewish, the Jewishness of any person is derivable from either parent and is expressed by participation in Jewish life.[5]

4. *Amarim* February 1981.
5. CCAR Minutes.

Discussion continued for two more years about the final wording of the Reform position. At its Los Angeles convention in 1983, the Central Conference of American Rabbis passed this resolution, which continues to be operative today:

> The children of one Jewish parent are presumed to be Jewish. The Jewish identity of the child must be affirmed through public and formal acts of identification with the Jewish faith and people. These acts include studying Torah, Bar/Bat Mitzvah, or Kabbalat HaTorah (Confirmation), entering into the Covenant (circumcision), and acquiring a Hebrew name.[6]

As a result of the meeting Shy attended in New York in 1981 and the official stance of the CCAR in 1983, Shy underscored these convictions:

1. Where Jewish law is contrary to facts, it should not be followed.

2. Reform Judaism has many contributions to make to a growing Jewish life that the other Jewish movements are unwilling to confront.

3. The growing rate of mixed marriages need not result in losses to the Jewish community if we are wise enough to guide the Jewish mate so that their children will be raised as Jews.[7]

Shy's liberalism was trail-blazing in his time. He modeled what it meant to be liberal— flexible, reflective, and open, yet committed to overarching principles— in this case, the preservation and growth of Judaism and the Jewish people.

6. CCAR Minutes.
7. *Amarim* 1981.

# 11

## Reaching Toward Social Justice

SHY CELEBRATED HIS EIGHTY-FIFTH birthday by writing *Zeldin's Way: Eighty-Five Stories for Eighty-Five Years* (2005). In the Epilogue, Shy tells readers:

> Since, as a young boy, my main texts were the stories of the Bible, it was the teachings of the prophets of Israel that moved me then and continue to move me today . . . So while I have performed the required priestly functions of a Reform rabbi, it is my role as an inheritor of the teachings of our prophets that I have truly cherished.[1]

In Chapter 5, I presented Shy's theology, influenced by Leo Baeck, Mordecai Kaplan, Abba Hillel Silver, and other rabbis. His theology was truly one of activism and partnership with God to respond to Torah's ethical summons. Shy also expressed his commitment to social justice in very concrete and realistic terms. In an interview, Shy gave voice to his concept of the role of the rabbi in the public arena:

> The most important role of the rabbi is to tell the truth as he sees it— fearlessly— in spite of consequences, even

---

1. *Zeldin's Way: Eighty-Five Stories for Eighty-Five Years,* 63.

if he gets bloodied. We can never be fence-sitters. On moral issues, we must be unequivocal.[2]

The values of Torah, not merely the Five Books of Moses but all of Jewish tradition, are the wellsprings of social justice. Shy knew sources and the tradition intimately. He learned the lessons of the Jewish experience in history. He applied those Jewish values and history lessons to lead the way on issues of justice and fairness. It is noteworthy that Shy did not ignore the requirements of the Jewish people while working for justice for the weak and disenfranchised in the general community and the world. Sometimes, the two categories, general and Jewish, abutted one another, and both were addressed.

Shortly following the Yom Kippur war in October of 1973, Arab oil states refused to sell oil to the United States and to Western European countries that supported Israel. At Stephen S. Wise Temple, Shy and the Social Action Committee decided to make their voice heard in opposition to the Arab oil embargo. People were requested to divest themselves of their Standard Oil credit cards. More than two hundred cards were returned to Standard Oil to protest the board chairman's "distortion of reality and dissemination of misrepresentations on the Middle East." Shy charged that Standard Oil's chairman, Otto N. Miller, had failed to consider Israel's role in the Middle East as well as pointedly omitting any mention of Israel in Standard Oil's policy letter to 302,000 stockholders and employees.

Shy and the Social Action Committee condemned Western countries like France and Britain, who yielded to Arab oil blackmail. Shy praised Holland and Portugal for standing up to Arab threats. He said that America should stand up to the blackmail. Shy was ahead of his time when he mused, "Perhaps this crisis will lead to the development of new sources of energy and to conserving fuel." He continued, "Jews will benefit when the rest of the world sees Arab chicanery." He also suggested that U.S. Jewry can

2. *Jewish Journal*, December 1995.

use economic pressure by not traveling to France or Britain and to countries that passively accept the Arab embargo.[3]

Black-Jewish relations since the 1960s and well into the late 1980s have been, at times, fulfilling and sometimes painful. Jews have long supported the NAACP, the work of Dr. Martin Luther King Jr., and his Southern Christian Leadership Conference. Young Jews sat in with Black demonstrators, rode freedom buses, and were on the front lines to register people to vote. Shy Zeldin ardently supported the Black-Jewish alliance.

The poison pill that almost killed Jewish sympathy for Black Americans was the articulate and charismatic Jesse Jackson. While Shy recognized Jackson's many talents as a leader of his people, he could not set aside his own Jewish loyalty. He remembered Jackson's derogatory reference to Jews as "Hymies." Jackson apologized and retracted his characterization of Jews. Shy, nevertheless, felt that Jackson, in his political campaigns of the 1980s, did not show himself to be a friend and ally of Israel. Jackson claimed that Israel joined (apartheid, white) South Africa in invading Angola. *The New Republic* (April 1998) reported that there was no basis, in fact, for Jackson's allegation. Shy felt certain that Jackson believed it was Israel alone who stood in the path to block a peace agreement with the Arabs. Despite all of Jackson's insensitive, insulting, and factually incorrect statements about Israel, Shy called on the Jewish community to "continue to work with the Black community on all of the causes that made them natural allies in the past."[4]

It was the speech of Nation of Islam elder Louis Farrakhan in Los Angeles in 1985, which further roiled the alliance between Black and Jewish communities. Farrakhan's speech called for greater economic opportunity for Blacks. He accused Jews of blocking the path to the hoped-for economic growth. He described Israel as a "wicked hypocrisy." Farrakhan stated publicly, "Don't push your six million down our throats when we lost one hundred million to slavery."[5]

3. *Amarim* January 1974.
4. *Jewish Journal,* June 1988.
5. *Los Angeles Times,* September 1985.

Shy and other Los Angeles rabbis called out leaders in the Black community for failing to condemn Farrakhan for his widely known antisemitism *before* he delivered the speech. In the weeks following Farrakhan's diatribe, Jews and Blacks began to work on repairing the inter-communal damage that was caused. Black leaders stated that their strategy was to reduce attention to Farrakhan by not saying anything prior to his speech. Shy, in no uncertain terms, faulted the Black community for not criticizing the Nation of Islam leader until after he spewed his hatred of Jews and Israel.

As a result of Shy's candor in forums of public debate and dialogue, a number of Black ministers, including Bishop H.H. Brookins of the A.M.Episcopal Church, admitted their error in failing to condemn Farrakhan upon his arrival in Los Angeles. Some Black leaders said they did not speak out in advance of Farrakhan's speech in the hope he would quietly moderate his antisemitic memes. Shy replied forthrightly, "An antisemite is an antisemite no matter what you do. Have you ever been able to change a Ku Klux Klanner? The only way you can deal with an individual of that sort is to expose him. You can't deny him freedom of speech, but certainly, you can make the entire community aware of the danger he spews forth."[6]

The outcome of discussions between Jewish and Black leaders was a renewal of productive contacts. Shy exchanged pulpits, inviting Black leaders to the pulpit of Stephen S. Wise Temple. He spoke at Praises of Zion Baptist Church in Watts. Stephen S. Wise Temple raised donations for a rummage sale for Praises of Zion Church in order that it could furnish and open its preschool. Such cooperative efforts bolstered the relationship between these two significant Los Angeles communities.

Three years later, things began to heat up again as a result of Jesse Jackson's candidacy for president. Shy, in an article in the *Jewish Journal*, suggested how the Jewish community should deal with Jesse Jackson:

6. *Los Angeles Times*, September 1985.

First, I believe American Jews ought to dialogue with him when he faces the realization that his lukewarm condemnations of antisemitism and his negative policies toward Israel have contributed to Jewish alienation. We ought to point out to him that his continuing rejection of Jewish nationalist aspirations will limit any political coalition he might want to forge for future elections. . . We should also continue to work with the black community on all of the causes that made us natural allies in the past.[7]

Shy and his congregation did that very thing when they joined with the NAACP in sponsoring a Health Day. Nineteen Jewish doctors and nineteen Black doctors examined two-hundred fifty Black people, most of whom had not had a medical exam for years, if at all. Another Health Day would be held in the Fairfax area to support Jews in the low-income neighborhood.[8]

One of the great displays of courage of Shy and several Los Angeles rabbis came as a result of California ballot Proposition 174. It was formally called The Education Voucher Initiative. The Initiative would have directed the state of California to provide $2,600 as a tuition voucher per child attending a private school. That plan would have removed over three billion dollars from the state's education budget for public schools. The expectation of those who proposed and supported Proposition 174 was that church and synagogue schools would hungrily accept state help via the voucher program.

Shy, together with colleagues Harold Schulweis, John Rosove and Jim Kaufman, flew in the face of the supporters of Prop. 174 by publicly opposing it. All of these rabbis had day schools in their congregations. It would have been in their interest to have parents receive state aid. Shy and the other rabbis refused. Shy stated that the diversion of dollars from the public schools would hurt society because it would be a death knell for them. He criticized giving state help to private schools, which might practice various forms

7. *Jewish Journal*, June 1988.
8. *Los Angeles Times*, 1986.

of discrimination based on religion, gender, or family income. All of the rabbis viewed the Voucher Initiative as seriously eroding the wall separating church and state. This they firmly opposed. Their stand was affirmed by the California voters when the voucher initiative was defeated at the polls in November of 1993.

Shy never shrank from addressing the issues of social justice. Together with the Social Action Committee, he initiated a "Critical Issues" speakers series. It included a debate on Proposition 6, known as The Gay Teachers Initiative, which would have prohibited gays and lesbians from teaching in public schools. This measure was defeated in 1978, demonstrating yet again the value of education and information. The Critical Issues series also addressed climate change, affirmative action vs. the quota system, and the plight of Soviet Jewry. In fact, talk turned to action when Stephen S. Wise Temple adopted two Soviet Jewish families who moved to Los Angeles from Odessa.

One may think that Shy's stature in his congregation and in the broader Jewish community might put him beyond criticism for his stands on issues of social justice. Not so! In 1976, Shy invited farmworker labor leader Cesar Chavez to sit on the bimah on Yom Kippur Day. This put a crack in the dam, which otherwise held back criticism. To his credit, Shy surveyed the congregation after the Holy Days about the liturgy and the sermons. He specifically addressed the matter of having Chavez on the pulpit:

> It evidently didn't sit well with too many members to have Cesar Chavez at the High Holy Days. However, many congregants are ignorant of the fact that the main difference between Judaism and other religions is that our faith is this-worldly, and justice and Judaism go hand in hand. In Judaism, the truly religious man is not only he who believes in God, prays and observes ritual, but also he who is the partner of God in helping to build his kingdom here on Earth.[9]

Some of Shy's critics argued that to speak about what they perceived to be political issues from the bimah transgresses the

9. *Amarim,* November 1976.

separation between church and state. Shy responded that this criticism misunderstands what separation of church and state means. While it does mean that the government should neither prohibit nor advocate religious expression, churches and synagogues are free to speak out on social ills, whether caused or tolerated by the government. If religious institutions were to remain silent in the face of societal evils or legislative shenanigans, "it would relegate them. . . to having little relevance to contemporary life."[10]

10. *Amarim,* November 1976.

# 12

# Pedagogy and Partnership

AMERICAN JEWISH SOCIOLOGY AND Rabbi Zeldin's decades-long vision of the vital necessity for extensive Jewish education combined to create the Stephen S. Wise Day School. In an article in *Amarim*,[1] Shy quoted a survey showing that twenty percent of college freshmen at Ivy League schools no longer considered themselves Jews. Another national survey found that thirty-three percent of Jewish college faculty did not identify themselves as Jews. This information was chilling to Shy. He had said many times that he wanted to be a rabbi to do something for the Jewish people. Aviva Feintech, an advocate of the Stephen S. Wise Parenting Center, was on the mark when she said, "Shy was all about the Jewish legacy and future generations."[2]

For Shy, all of this pointed in one direction: quality Jewish education. He understood the attraction of offering a nursery school, and he led the temple to create it. The school grew to an enrollment of one hundred twenty-five little ones, the largest Jewish nursery school in Los Angeles. Dafna Presnell, a dynamic educator, took over the nursery school. When congregants Marilyn Brown and Norma Freeman approached Shy with the idea of establishing a

1. *Amarim*, Stephen S. Wise Synagogue bulletin, February 1971.
2. Interview: Aviva Feintech.

Parenting Center with a Mommy and Me class, the Rabbi was receptive and encouraging. Soon, the program grew so large that it required a building to house it. Marilyn, Norma, and their families donated gifts to bring the building to reality. Shy thought if Judaism would speak to the needs of contemporary generations, we need to educate young Jews to make them learned and wise. He used the metaphor of musicians in a symphony orchestra. "If," said Shy, "America is a symphony orchestra, Jews must play their part. We need to be knowledgeable and literate to do so."[3]

Shy felt encouraged by the outstanding Jewish educator, Shlomo Bardin. In 1965, Bardin wrote a report entitled *The Case for Jewish Preparatory School in Los Angeles*. Here is an excerpt:

> . . .we need to create quality institutions of education where the best and brightest of our children can have their learning laced through with the insights and values which Judaism possesses and which it can indeed bring to bear on all knowledge. American Jewry can and will afford a Jewish Exeter or Jewish Andover where the finest classical education can be fused with finest classics of Judaism.[4]

Stephen S. Wise Temple was founded in 1964. Even from its earliest days, the congregation provided Jewish education through weekly religious and Hebrew school classes of two hours duration. The school met in the classrooms of Leo Baeck Temple. Providing space for the Stephen S. Wise School was an act of fraternal kindness by Rabbi Leonard Beerman and the Leo Baeck congregation.

For Shy, despite the quality of his synagogue's religious school, part-time Jewish education was insufficient to mold knowledgeable, committed, creative young Jews with leadership skills. His dream for deeper Jewish education was congruent with the expressions of Dr. Bardin, Rabbi Mordecai Kaplan, and Rabbi Abraham Heschel.

---

3. Zeldin, *What This Modern Jew Believes,* 168.

4. Quoted by Rabbi Balfour Brickner in "Blueprint for Jewish Survival." Publication date uncertain.

The Stephen S. Wise Temple Elementary Day School opened in 1976, just prior to the Congregation's Bar/Bat Mitzvah anniversary. As students entered the fifth grade, Shy enthusiastically encouraged the building and development of a sixth through ninth-grade middle school.

Shy was the dreamer of the Stephen S. Wise Middle School as well as being the non-pareil fundraiser. He was also aware that he could not achieve his goals without capable, competent partners. His solid, thoughtful, and sensitive disciple, Rabbi Eli Herscher, led the synagogue staff. He was present for congregants. Eli's leadership made it possible for Shy to put all of his own energy and attention into building the schools he envisioned.

Lowell Milken was a partner and good friend of Shy. Lowell grew up at a synagogue in the San Fernando Valley. He always felt that the one-day-a-week school program was sorely lacking. He hungered for more learning and greater depth. When Lowell, in his late twenties, met Shy, he realized the Stephen S. Wise Day School was what he wanted for his own kids. Lowell and Shy became close friends over the years. Lowell felt that he and Shy were equal partners in expanding the Day School. From the standpoint of both education and business, Lowell realized that he and Shy learned from one another.

When the Conservative movement's Einstein Academy was in a financial tailspin and could not pay its teachers, David Smith, a former president of Stephen S. Wise Temple, went to Shy to discuss saving the Academy. Lowell Milken indicated that the Milken Foundation would be willing to back a community high school. They approached local rabbis to see if a joint venture on a high school could happen. It turned out that, of the rabbis in attendance at the meeting, only Shy backed the idea of the high school. Shy and Lowell took on the Einstein Academy with its budget difficulties. The beginning of the Stephen S. Wise High School with the Einstein Academy in its final year became a reality. At the outset, the school was housed in the dormitory at the University of Judaism. The opening year of the Stephen S. Wise High School was 1991. By 1994, the school moved to a new forty-five-million-dollar campus just to the west of the San Diego freeway. The initial plan was to build three buildings, with a fourth building to be built later. Shy thought about what a fourth building would cost a few years down the road. Shy told Lowell he needed the fourth building at the same time as the other three. Shy asked Lowell to backstop the building number four. Lowell agreed, provided Shy would raise the rest of the money. Shy undertook the commitment and succeeded at that challenge.

Ken Ruby, z"l, was another partner of great know-how and dedication. Rabbi Yoshi, the current senior rabbi of Stephen S. Wise Temple,
said of him:

> Ken was an exceptional leader and quintessential mensch. I learned so much working with him on our most recent building projects, the Katz Family Pavilion and the Aaron Milken Center. Ken's wisdom and experience can be seen not only throughout our campus but throughout our Jewish community.[5]

For years, Ken chaired the building committee and was president of the Congregation 1991–1993. He was a close, cherished friend of Shy. It was Ken who negotiated the purchase of the High School property. He, among others, was able to turn Shy's vision into reality.

Metuka Benjamin had been Shy's strong right arm as the developer and Director of Education of the Stephen S. Wise Day Schools. Rabbi Yoshi Zweiback, who had been Director of Education at Temple Beth Am in Palo Alto, California, was brought on to succeed Metuka in 2012.[6] Not long after Rabbi Yoshi's engagement as Director of Education, the school's board approved a full separation of the High School from the Wise Temple's day school system. The rationale for this decision was a concern that members of other congregations feared the Stephen S. Wise High School would

5. Quoted in Milken Community High School's announcement of death of Ken Ruby.

6. Rabbi Zweiback is currently the Senior Rabbi of what is now called Wise Temple.

pull kids and families from their synagogues and that registration at Wise would be met with communal resistance. Rabbi Herscher went down to Shy's retirement home in the desert to inform him of the decision to separate the high school from Stephen S. Wise Temple. Shy understood the separation and said, "Look at the gift we gave the community." The school was the result of his dreams and his labor, yet he acquiesced to the plan. In his view, regardless of the administrative structure and the school's name, Shy believed that a "Jewish high school education will determine whether there is a viable non-Orthodox future in the U.S."[7]

When the Stephen S. Wise High School opened in 1991, the student body in its first year was one- hundred sixty-five. As part of its philosophy of knowing students personally as individuals, all incoming students were interviewed. This helped to determine the interests and strengths of students as well as their seriousness and sense of community.[8] Today, the Milken Community Day School serves seven- hundred fifty students, including middle and high school grades six through twelve.

Shortly before Shy's ninetieth birthday, Eli recorded an interview with him. Eli asked Shy, "You began the work to establish the high school when you were seventy. Did you ever think you were taking on too much?"

Shy answered, "I was too damned arrogant to consider that! I always knew the high school would work. Failure never entered my mind."

For Shy to call himself "arrogant" was more likely to be a sign of his own humility. To be sure, Shy was neither arrogant nor meek. He well knew his strengths and shortcomings. He was a person of equanimity, a man who could keep his balance, part realist and part visionary. As to this second quality, Shy was an analytic thinker and a calculated risk-taker. He could see success down the road and lead others to view it as well.

Shy had, of course, many talents. Singing on key and melodically was not among them. Shy did, nevertheless, appreciate music

7. Zeldin, *What This Modern Jew Believes,* 164.
8. To learn details of the school's philosophy and goal, see Appendix.

in services and in student education. He encouraged his cantor, Nate Lam, to bring all styles of Jewish music into worship services. Shy inspired Nate, as well as music aficionado Lowell Milken, to create a music archive at Stephen S. Wise Temple. They founded the Milken Archive of Jewish Music. Today, there are more than seven hundred recordings housed at U.C.L.A. in the Milken Center for Music of the American Jewish Experience.

In the mid-1980s, Shy wrote:

> The Stephen S. Wise Temple's Day School program of Jewish and general studies reflects the conviction that a young person's total identity derives from both our Jewish and American heritage. Our staff—teachers, counselors, clergy, custodians—works together to create a learning environment that is pleasant, challenging, and responsive to the needs of young people and their families.[9]

Shy, his fellow clergy, the education staff, and all their supporters accomplished this goal at the highest level.

9. Stephen S. Wise Temple Archives.

# 13

## A Passion for Israel

SHY VIEWED ISRAEL'S EXISTENCE as a miracle. The miracle of the Jewish state was the wonder of what Zionists created in the Land of Israel. They returned to the Jewish ancestral homeland, built up the country, and developed institutions necessary for an eventual independent Jewish nation. All of this effort and its successful result was brought about by dreamers and doers, not by a heaven-sent messiah. For Shy, the United Nations' affirmation of a Jewish state in part of the Land of Israel was what his father, Morris, his mentor, Rabbi Stephen S. Wise, and he himself worked to realize.

It was no wonder then that Shy and Florence traveled to Israel with their two-year-old son, Joel, in 1949. They toured the country and saw sights that were familiar to them from photos and, from their Bible study and their imagination. They tucked baby Joel into the baskets of the bicycles they rode to see the country from an intimate perspective.

The idea of *making aliyah*,[1] settling in Israel, was very much on their minds. This dream was not to become a reality. Shy realized that there was no role for a Reform rabbi in a Jewish state under whose auspices the Orthodox rabbinate had sole Jewish religious authority. Shy was committed to being a Reform rabbi,

1. Making aliyah literally means "going up." Settling in Israel has always been viewed as an ascent physically and spiritually.

to working for and guiding liberal Jews. He knew in his innermost being that he could do more for his people, those in the U.S. and those in Israel, by serving Jewish communities and congregations in America.

Shy was well aware of the crucial and deep connection which existed between Israeli and American Jews. He told his associate, Rabbi Eli Herscher, "I knew during the War of Independence that if Israel lost, American Jews would be lost. If Israel falls, Reform and Conservative Judaism would not survive."[2] Thus, Shy was and always remained a defender of and advocate for Israel. During the Six-Day War of 1967, Shy called a meeting that was to be held in the large Sanctuary of Westwood United Methodist Church. Jews filled the cavernous auditorium and pledged substantial donations to support Israel in its time of need. In a similar gathering during the Yom Kippur War of 1973, Shy raised in one afternoon $200,000, the equivalent of $1,500,00 in 2024 dollars. While the fundraising events were precipitated by crises, Stephen S. Wise Temple also raised money to bring sick Israeli children to the U.S. for medical treatment not available in Israel.

Shy had an overarching policy with regard to Israel: do not criticize Israel publicly. Shy saw Israel's many challenges and flaws. Because he was especially mindful of the "schriers" of which Israel has a plethora, he disavowed those shrill public critics of Israel. He stated from the pulpit and in print that what he deemed excessive public criticism of Israel by left-wing Jewish groups was treasonous and harmful to the Jewish people. He leveled such a view against Breira and the New Jewish Agenda, two ardent pro-peace groups. Shy said the New Jewish Agenda was neither new nor Jewish.

Shy advocated private communication with Israeli leaders to let them know of American Jewish concerns. He made sure to convey to Israeli leaders behind the scenes that liberal Jews, Reform, and Conservative, comprised the largest of the American Jewish factions. He emphasized to Israeli leaders the imperative

2. The two liberal branches of Judaism identify strongly with Jewish peoplehood and with Israel more than on traditional observance of rabbinic commandments, the core of Orthodox identity.

not to shatter the mutual support between the Israeli and diaspora communities.

Often, Shy was able to offer his constructive criticisms privately to Israeli leaders. Stephen S. Wise Temple was known to be the second largest non-Orthodox synagogue in the U.S. Israeli leaders were aware of the day schools and athletic facilities. They wanted to meet Shy and see the campus of the synagogue-community center he built. Students impressed Israeli visitors with their knowledge of spoken Hebrew and Hebrew songs. Among the Israeli leaders who visited and spoke at the Temple over the years were Teddy Kollek (Mayor of Jerusalem), Benny Begin (Knesset member, son of Menachem), Moshe Arens (Defense Minister), Yitzchak Shamir (Prime Minister), Yitzchak Rabin (Prime Minister). Shy was an important voice, and his listeners came to understand more clearly the imperative of close American-Jewish and Israeli ties.

Shy made his avid support of Israel clear from the pulpit. He did so as well in opinion columns he wrote for the *Los Angeles Jewish Journal.*

Shy remonstrated with the editor of the Journal for "Israel bashing." The editor claimed that Israel was an obstacle to peace in the Middle East. He stated more than once that Israel is losing its soul. Shy strongly argued against the editor's view. The editor accused Shy of being "thin-skinned." Shy denied any such description. He claimed that those who write or demonstrate publicly against Israel, though they say they love Israel, are divisive in the Jewish community. In 1988, Shy said the secular press is extremely critical, if not negative, of Israel. Shy felt the Jewish press should not be neutral and should defend Israel.

Despite Shy's strong, clear position, he recognized the complexity and nuance of Israel's situation. He thought that Jewish unity and mutual tolerance among Jewish groups and parties had to be a precursor to a comprehensive peace. He opined that in any peace negotiations, Israel must move slowly and cautiously because the security of the State of Israel must be the priority. He distrusted Hamas, and felt with them there could be no territorial compromise. With regard to Jewish settlements in Gaza and the West Bank, Shy asked theoretically: "Arabs live in Israel; why should not Jews live in Arab territory?"

Shy believed U.S. Jewry should support the Israeli government in four areas:

1. Jerusalem must remain undivided.

2. Israel must reject a return to the difficult-to-defend 1967 armistice lines.

3. There can be no Palestinian state in the West Bank.

4. The Jordan River must be maintained as Israel's eastern boundary.

It must be noted that in 2008, Likud Prime Minister Ehud Olmert, in discussions with Palestinian leaders, came to a compromise peace plan that contradicted the views of most Israelis and Shy's view. Yet in 1988, when Secretary of State George Schultz decided to open talks with Arafat and the PLO, Shy joined Rabbis Beerman, Schulweis, and others in support of the Schultz initiative. Indeed, there was significant rabbinic skepticism about Arafat's sincerity. It was Shy's view that Arafat was acting for tactical gain rather than out of a true commitment to peace. Hindsight tells us that Shy was correct, and talks went nowhere.

Shy took a visible, courageous stand regarding Jonathan Pollard, an American Naval Intelligence employee who was arrested in 1985 for passing military intelligence to Israel. The U.S. government claimed that though Israel was a close ally, Pollard compromised U.S. security by sharing information on Arab militaries with Israel. Initially, Pollard was promised a lenient sentence in exchange for his cooperation in the case and for a guilty plea. The U.S. government reneged. Pollard was sentenced to life in prison, an unprecedented term since others who spied for American allies received two to four years punishment.

Many American Jews were appalled and frightened by the Pollard case. The last thing U.S. Jews wanted was to be accused of having a dual loyalty to their country and Israel. At first, most of U.S. Jewry remained relatively silent. Yet others felt there was more than a hint of antisemitism in Pollard's sentence. In 1991, in Los Angeles, the first pro-Pollard rally was held. Shy, before six hundred people at Stephen S. Wise Temple, said that the U.S. government double-crossed Pollard. He said that U.S. Jews and the American government shared the guilt for Pollard's ongoing imprisonment. He chastised U.S. Jews for being so meek and afraid of the dual loyalty charge. It took close to twenty-five additional years until Pollard was released and made Aliyah.

Shy not only sought to defend Israel but found a pathway to make Israel more democratic and pluralistic. That route was through the Association of Reform Zionists of America, or its acronym, ARZA.[3] ARZA itself is a remarkable creation. The Reform movement was on record as being anti-Zionist from 1885 until 1937.[4] Forty-one years passed from that time until ARZA was established as the official arm of Reform Zionism. Rabbi Roland B. Gittelsohn was one of the early visionaries who created ARZA. He was also its founding president in 1977.

In 1978, Shy advocated to his congregation that its members join and support ARZA. He explained that ARZA nourished an intrinsic, organic relationship between Israel and the diaspora. He believed that ARZA stood for activism, intellectual fervor, the fight for justice, and Jewish religious pluralism in Israel. ARZA worked to create a Jewish state of equality for all its citizens.

As with so many other projects, Shy pushed ARZA intensively. He held a special ARZA Shabbat in December of 1978. He sent Dr. Charlene Hyde as the Stephen S. Wise Temple representative to the first ARZA convention in Washington, D.C. ARZA grew and blossomed into being the leading party in the World Zionist Organization, comprising forty percent of its membership. ARZA received from the United Jewish Appeal proportional funds based on the size of its membership. Those funds support the Israel Movement for Progressive Judaism, which sustains Reform schools, synagogues, the Israel Religious Action Center, and many

3. ARZA is also "to the land!" in Hebrew.

4. In 1937 the Central Conference of American Rabbis voted to affirm Reform support for Zionism.

other programs. ARZA and all its contributions have fostered the growth of Reform Judaism in Israel, which currently counts fifty-four congregations. After all these years of pioneering, growth, and development, Shy could be a Reform rabbi in Israel as he once dreamed.

Two other highlights of Shy's life regarding Israel made him shine with energy and joy. In 1987, the American Friends of the Hebrew University presented him with the first Martin Buber Award in Jewish education. It was a fitting acknowledgment from Israel's premier university to America's premier Jewish educator and school builder.

The second and symbolic highlight occurred when Shy led a tour to Israel with eighty congregants to celebrate his eightieth birthday. When we love a person, an experience, or an environment, we want to share that contact with others. In Pirkei Avot (5:24), Rabbi Judah ben Tema tells us that while human life is seventy years, reaching eighty is a special gift of strength. Shy absorbed special strength and fulfillment from being in the land of Israel and the state of Israel. The eighty people who accompanied him received his strength there as well.

# 14

## Our Life Is Our Eulogy

SHY AND FLORENCE MADE sure for years to have a place for a quiet escape from the demands of congregational life. At different times, they rented apartments in Oxnard, Simi Valley, and the Palm Springs area. These hide-aways gave Shy and Florence cherished couple time as well as regular opportunities for Shy to play golf. Eventually, the Zeldins bought a home in Sun City with a golf course view. That home was the place of their active retirement.

The Zeldins had a life of success and fulfillment. They also encountered personal medical challenges. In 1995, Florence was diagnosed with bone cancer, which necessitated a knee replacement. She also underwent chemotherapy. Florence entered remission with no recurrence of cancer. During this period, Shy was with her one hundred percent with his love, caring, and energy. He even made it his business to learn how to run their dishwasher. Florence did not find walking with an artificial knee easy or pain-free. With Shy's encouragement, Florence just toughed it out with neither a cane nor a crutch. Stephen S. Wise Temple gifted the Zeldins with a hot tub to support Flo's recuperation. Flo, ten months older than Shy, was diagnosed in 2011 with congenital heart failure. She died in May of 2012 at age 92. Shy said that the passing of his beloved life partner was the hardest thing that he ever had to deal with.

Two facets of Shy's later years sustained him: long-time friends and grandchildren. From both, he drew *nachas,* joy, and fulfillment. There was a group of friends from Stephen S. Wise Temple who had also retired in Sun City. Most of them had known each other for decades. Those friends encouraged Shy to lead Friday evening services in the desert on a monthly basis. He and Florence also went to Los Angeles from time to time for special occasions. These activities made it possible for Shy to tell an interviewer, "I am the oldest practicing rabbi in the United States." Eventually, Shy convinced Hillel Cohen, Rabbi Emeritus of Congregation Emanu-El of San Bernardino, to lead services once or twice a month in Sun City. Shy continued to speak and to teach in the desert. One of the people in Shy's circle of friends suggested having a Friday evening Shabbat dinner at Wendy's in Palm Desert. The management enthusiastically accommodated the group. Attendees brought in Shabbat candles and sang the blessing. Grape juice and challah graced the tables. Everyone participated in the appropriate blessings. Shy was a regular member of the group. Everyone loved the Wendy's Shabbat dinner custom. It became an extended family, a mutually supportive community. It was unique and inspiring, with a YouTube video of it for anyone to watch.

The passing of group members who were close to one another for decades impacted the surviving retirees. Shy felt these losses deeply. He was especially saddened by the death of Sylvia Hershenson. Sylvia and her husband, Abe, were extremely generous donors to Stephen S. Wise Temple. They were faithful supporters of Shy and Florence. Sylvia was born in British Palestine, lived there as a child, and spoke Hebrew. These elements of her background drew Shy to her so that her death was like the death of a sister.

Shy died on January 26, 2018, a little less than half a year before his ninety-eighth birthday. At his funeral service, which filled the sanctuary and its extensions at Stephen S. Wise Temple, two of Shy's grandchildren delivered a joint eulogy. They spoke for all five of the Zeldin grandchildren. The joy Shy received from

his grandchildren was the zenith of his life. These are the words of
Gabe Zeldin and Sivan Zakai:

Gabe:

Many of you are here today to pay tribute to Rabbi Zeldin.
Some of you are here to honor Shy. We are here on behalf
of the people lucky enough to call him Grandpa Shy.

Sivan:

We've been thinking about the legacy that Grandpa Shy
has left the 15 of us— his grandchildren, our spouses,
and his great-grandchildren. Noam has inherited Grandpa Shy's love of stories and storytelling.

Gabe:

Sasha has inherited Grandpa's interest in education.

Sivan:

Oren has Grandpa's love of basketball.

Gabe:

And Sivan has his fluency with words.

Sivan:

Gabe inherited Grandpa Shy's ability to solve puzzles and
his ability to speak in public without notes.

Gabe:

It is the last trait— the ability to stand in front of a room
of people, speak for minutes (or sometimes hours) on
end, and never once refer to a single written note— that
was one of Grandpa Shy's most impressive traits, and we
are both going to talk about it today.

Sivan:

To start, I will pay tribute to him by telling you about the
greatest legacy that he left us and, at the same time, sharing with you his not-so secret trick for delivering lengthy
sermons without even a scrap of paper to refer to.

*Fun.*

Grandpa Shy was a fun-loving man with many hobbies.
Chief among those was golf. Each of his grandchildren

and great-grandchildren learned from a young age the joy of riding in Grandpa Shy's golf cart, and we greatly anticipated the day we actually got to learn to drive it. Golf cart driving lessons with Grandpa Shy functioned much like a personality test for the daredevil (Oren) or vigilant (Sasha) within us and would be brought to the fore the first moment that Grandpa Shy said, "It's time to put your foot on the gas pedal."

Golf itself was a mirror of Grandpa Shy's own personality. He spent countless hours with Gabe and Oren on the golf course, teaching them about golf and about patience. Yet each time he himself made a bad shot, he would chastise himself with, "Come on, Zeldin!"

That's a line he also used when playing chess, another one of his hobbies. When I was a child and broke the sad news that I did not share his love of golf, he quickly pivoted and tried to teach me chess. Alas, I was never the chess partner he sought (after all, he was a ranked chess player!), but Eytan was patient enough to learn the chess moves I never could, and together they spent long afternoons hunched over the chess board.

Grandpa also loved talking philosophy, and for that, he found a wonderful companion in Noam. They would go on long walks and discuss politics, theology, or theories on how to live a good life. I was never privy to those conversations, but whatever they settled on clearly worked.

*Admiring.*

Grandpa Shy had the opportunity to meet with a lot of dignitaries during his life. If you looked at the pictures of Grandpa Shy with the Dalai Lama or Grandpa Shy with President Clinton or Grandpa Shy with Prime Minister Shamir or Prime Minister Rabin, you might think: in comparison with them, what have I accomplished?

But that's not how Grandpa Shy saw it. He looked at each of his grandchildren, and especially his great-grandchildren, and believed them to be highly accomplished people. To him, Alina merited a place in the Guinness Book of World Records for her boundless energy. Stav and Ido warranted Mensa membership because, even as babies, they were bilingual. Evan deserved a gold medal for curiosity. And the way he kvelled over the fact that Eytan and Ilan were enrolled as students at Wise School (only the best for the best) and that Liam was part of the Hebrew Immersion program of the Wise ECC (another brilliant Hebrew speaker!) In his eyes, these accomplishments were just as important as those of Heads of State.

*Munificent.*

Meaning more generous than is usual or necessary, perfectly describes our grandfather, who wanted nothing more than for everyone around him to be happy and who was willing to give whatever he had to make our happiness possible. "Anything, up to half my kingdom," he would say, quoting the Book of Esther. And then he'd put a bill or a check in our hand to make sure that we had enough to cover the plane fare or the gas money we spent to come and visit him, not wanting us to be put out even for the pleasure of his company.

Grandpa Shy was also generous with his attention. Whenever you would come to a Friday night evening service that he led, at the end of the service, there would be a line of people queuing up to speak with him. But if we, his grandchildren, were at the service, no matter how long the line was and no matter who it included, he would make a point of saying hello to us first. He made time for everyone, but he made sure we knew that we were a priority.

*Inclusive.*

When I was in preschool, Grandpa Shy came to visit my class one day. I ran up to him, according to my family lore, threw my arms around him, and said, "I love you, Grandpa Shy." So did my childhood friend Lisa Lewis, who also always called him Grandpa Shy. Thinking it was a social protocol, the entire class of preschool children then ran up to him and, throwing their arms around his legs, echoed, "We love you, Grandpa Shy!"

To a casual observer, it might seem strange for a room full of children to call the senior rabbi "Grandpa," but anyone who knew him well understood that while he was *our* grandfather, he was willing and able to include others as his grandchildren as well.

To my maternal cousins Mason, Justin, and Sawyer Kroll, and to our friend Max Borenstein, he was never anything other than Grandpa Shy. When Igor, Dusty, and Noga each joined the family, he considered them grandchildren on equal footing with those of us who had been in the family for a long time.

With each of these grandchildren, he shared the special Grandpa shy kiss: a kiss on the right cheek, then one on the left, then one in the middle of the forehead.

*Lesson of the Day.*

When we were children, Grandpa Shy always gave us a Lesson of the Day, though in truth, he tended to recycle the same three:

1) Eat your fruits and vegetables.

   Then he'd say, "What do you call a 100-year-old man who has eaten broccoli every day of his life? Old!"

2) Always remember the rule of 72.

   For those of you who have never had a Grandpa Shy Lesson of the Day or a financial advisor, divide 72 by the interest rate of your investment, and—presto— that's how long it will take your money to double.

3) Learn to love the things you have to do.

   While this was Grandpa Shy's most profound lesson, it was also a reminder of lesson one: eat your fruits and vegetables. It turns out that while Grandpa Shy ate broccoli every single day (what do you call a man who has eaten broccoli for 97 years?), he did not, in fact, like broccoli.

As we got older, or maybe just as he got older, the lessons of the day began to harken back to his own childhood as a yeshiva bocher.

*Yehalelucha acherim v'lo picha*, he would teach. Let others praise you and not your own mouth. But then he would switch it and say: *Yehalelucha acherim. V'lo? Picha!* Let others praise you. And if not? Your own mouth!

Or he'd teach, *Tov chaver karov meach rachok.* It's better to have a nearby friend than a far-away brother. But then he'd insist: *Tov chaver karov. Meach rachok!* It's good to have a nearby friend. But that's far from having a brother!

*Ya da da.*

For this one, I'll need the help of Cantor Emma.

This is Grandpa Shy's favorite niggun, the song that he sang to each of his grandchildren (and, while he could, his great-grandchildren) when we were babies. Grandpa Shy had a magical way with babies, and he would whisk away a fussy or overtired one and sing this niggun over and over again until the baby fell asleep.

For his grandchildren, this niggun will always carry Grandpa Shy's love and a sense of serenity.

Put it all together:

F for Fun
A for Admiring
M for Munificent
I for Inclusive
L for his Lesson of the Day
Y for the Ya Da Da of his niggun
F-A-M-I-L-Y

That was Grandpa Shy's trick for speaking from the bimah without notes. He'd always come up with a mnemonic and spell his way through the sermon.

And that is the greatest legacy that he left us. He always said that, with all the buildings that he built, with all the institutions that he founded, with all the programs he created, his family was his greatest legacy. Thank you, Grandpa Shy.

Shy had a sweet soul. He reached out to help others cultivate the potential of their own souls. He added much sweetness to the spirit of the Jewish people and the world. His memory will remain a guide and a sweet blessing.

# 15

# Epilogue

RABBI ABRAHAM JOSHUA HESCHEL wrote: "We need fewer text-books and more text people who teach students by their personal warmth, practice and morality."

Shy's life and rabbinate illustrated Heschel's understanding of the needs of the Jewish people in America. When a seventh-grade student showed up at the temple for a first middle school youth group gathering, and no other students attended, Shy shot baskets with the young man for an hour. Shy and Flo made it a practice to show up at B'nai Mitzvah celebrations to honor families and to add to their *simcha*. Shy was a moral giant, a leader who always taught Jewish truths about social issues.

Shy was a text person. He was an activist. He taught with intellectual fervor. He fought for justice, democracy, Israel, and pluralism. He demonstrated in his goals and accomplishments his conviction that a creative and dynamic liberal Jewish community could flourish in the United States.

Shy Zeldin was known and admired around the country. A few envied his vast abilities and talents. All agreed on his sincerity, his integrity, and his loving devotion to the Jewish people.

In Los Angeles County, his influence was impactful and challenging. Whether as founding dean of the west coast branch of Hebrew Union College-Jewish Institute of Religion, director of the western office of the Union of American Hebrew Congregations, or senior rabbi of two outstanding Reform synagogues, Shy imprinted the community with his vision. He was indeed a text person and a *zisse Neshama,* a sweet soul.

# Afterword
## What Choice Did I Have?

Rabbi Eli Herscher

Paul Citrin's loving remembrance of Rabbi Isaiah Zeldin is not only testament to an extraordinary life of inspired leadership, but perhaps even more importantly, a potent reminder of how the endless possibilities for a vibrant and hopeful Jewish life in America can be realized *only by virtue of such leadership*. When Theodor Herzl imagined a future Jewish State – considered by many to be a dream unlikely ever to be fulfilled – the visionary Zionist declared, "it you will it, it is no dream." Shy Zeldin similarly believed in the act of willfully transforming vision into reality for the American Jewish community.   Over the many decades in which I worked with Shy virtually every day, it was only in the rarest of moments that I saw him tire.   As he dreamed and built a unique institution — with new buildings going up almost every year to meet the growing needs of our schools, and new and innovative programs to inspire a community that ultimately grew to serve some ten thousand Jews of all ages — I have no doubt that there were days that he must have been utterly exhausted.  How could that not be so, given the passionate energy that he devoted to every moment of his efforts on behalf of Stephen S. Wise Temple?  But he rarely, if ever, allowed fatigue to stop him because, I believe, he knew at the core of his being that his unique contributions were both urgently needed and necessary.  Indeed, Shy was driven by a vision of Judaism and a love of the Jewish People and Israel that allowed little time for rest. In 1975, when he invited me to work alongside him, he cautioned me, "Eli, I work twice as hard as any Rabbi, and I expect you to do the same." I took him at his word. Shy lived and worked as if a vibrant and viable Jewish future lay squarely on his shoulders and in his hands — that nothing should or could stop him from ensuring that future.

What inspired his tenacity, his depth of conviction, his confidence?

Early in my own rabbinic career, I asked Shy what had moved him to become a rabbi. He told me of the day in 1933 when his father had taken him to hear Rabbi Stephen S. Wise speak at an anti-Nazi rally at Madison Square Garden. In telling the story, Shy imitated Wise's accent, his dramatically deep baritone, as well as the heightened volume of his mentor's voice, as Wise railed against the imminent dangers to the Jews of Europe. It was at that moment, Shy told me, that he decided that if a rabbi had that kind of power to speak on behalf of the Jewish people and to lead with that kind of passion, then he, too, must become a rabbi. He was all of 13-years-old when his sense of purpose and power and drive were born.

And when he was called to lead, Shy found Jews who were more than ready to follow him, who resonated to his vision, as well as to the natural gifts of his personality. I became one among them when I first met him while still in rabbinical school. In 1973, on the Friday immediately following the outbreak of the Yom Kippur war, I knew that Rabbi Zeldin was the singular voice among Los Angeles Jewish leaders whom I needed to hear. Many others felt the same. Stephen Wise, still a relatively young congregation, was packed that Shabbat evening by Jews who needed to find comfort, inspiration, and a call to action on behalf of Israel. Indeed, whenever Israel was endangered over the decades, Shy invariably brought his passionate love and commitment to the Stephen Wise *bima*. The love of Israel, of Judaism, of the Jewish People, were at the core of his being, and he awakened that love in everyone who heard him speak.

Shy Zeldin was an immensely powerful teacher of the core Jewish narrative. When he taught Jewish values and his passion for justice, the words he spoke came from his heart and, so, entered our hearts. This was true in the classroom, as it was from the pulpit. His speaking style was mesmerizing, as was his content. When he taught Bible, he brought its personalities to life. I recall the High Holy Day sermon he delivered in which he told the story of David. He dramatized the King's triumphs, as well as his downfall, his loves as well as his sorrows. He made you feel as if he knew David personally, and so he made you feel you knew David as well. Few could bring Jewish learning into the lives of his students in the vibrant ways that Shy did. He was the consummate teacher, and the master storyteller. And, as Rabbi Citrin has beautifully portrayed, he lived a storied rabbinic career.

Around the time that Shy turned 90, he and I shared a lunch at which I asked him to reflect, not only on *what* he had created, but more, on how he never seemed to entertain even a moment of doubt about the certain success of any project he undertook. Although there were nay-sayers to many of those projects, Shy was never held back. Many rabbis would have considered the risks, financial and otherwise, inherent in creating a day school and, at the age of 70, taking on the enormous challenge of building a Jewish High School. What was, I asked, the source of his optimism in undertaking one major project after another? He only needed a moment to consider my question. "Really, Eli," he responded, "what *choice* did I have? What choice did I have!" When it came to the needs of Jewish life at that moment in our history, and as he looked to both the challenges and creative possibilities of the Jewish future, when it came to enriching the quality of Jewish education for generations of Jewish children, when it came to the safety and well-being of Israel and the flourishing of American Jewish life, Shy jumped at every opportunity to lead. He truly — indeed, passionately and with his whole being — believed that he had no choice but to do the work he was not only capable of doing, but that he was destined to do.

And so he did it. . . with an incomparable singleness of purpose. He worked with a combination of zeal balanced by deep thoughtfulness, as well as with enormous joy. I've rarely known anyone who exuded the kind of joy in his work that Shy Zeldin experienced every day. (It was an infectious joy. . . and I admit to having been infected.) I still remember his telling me of driving up to the Temple one day with his beloved Florence — whom he knew as Tsippora/Tsip — seated beside him. With a sense of wonder, he gazed at everything he had dreamed, at everything he had created on his mountaintop and said, "pinch me, Tsip, pinch me."

When Paul asked me to compose an Afterword to his beautiful narrative, I considered what "afterword" might mean in the story of Rabbi Isaiah Zeldin. What words might come *"after"* such a life of inspired Jewish leadership? Ultimately, the truest afterword will be written within the Jewish lives yet to be, the generations who will receive the blessings Shy gave them as a great gift, his extraordinary legacy.

Isaiah and Florence Zeldin, 1943

(l. to r.) Michael, Isaiah, Joel, Florence, 1958

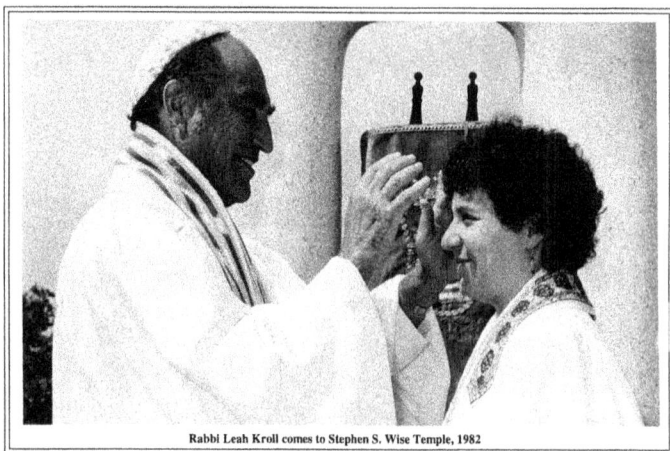
Rabbi Leah Kroll comes to Stephen S. Wise Temple, 1982

Rabbi Isaiah Zeldin
and
Stephen S. Wise Temple
Educational Director
Metuka Benjamin
1990

Rabbi Isaiah Zeldin
and
Shimon Peres,
then Foreign Minister of Israel,
1988

Rabbi Isaiah Zeldin
and
Israeli Prime Minister
Yitzhak Rabin
1992

King Hussein of Jordan
and
Rabbi Isaiah Zeldin
1995

# Appendix

## Educational Goals and Philosophy of the Milken Community School

### LIST OF THE FOUNDING MEMBERS OF STEPHEN S. WISE TEMPLE, 1964

a vision of the future...

### THE MASTER PLAN

We are investing in a High School. Stephen S. Wise Temple is the only Reform congregation in the United States sponsoring a community full-day high school. Because of the growing excellence of our program, we now draw students from many Conservative congregations, other Reform congregations, some Orthodox congregations, and a great many unaffiliated Jewish families.

We have invested our energies and our finances in the purchase of a 10-acre site just across the 405 freeway on Mulholland Drive, less than 1/4 of a mile away from our present 18-acre campus. On our new site, we will have 33 regular classrooms, science labs, language labs, a computer lab, a library, music and creative arts rooms, an auditorium for performances and lectures, a Beit Midrash for prayer and study, a cafeteria, gym, soccer field, basketball courts, and other athletic facilities.

We believe the time has come for the Reform and Conservative Movements to help sponsor a secondary school that will prepare future informed Jewish leaders who participate in all walks of life, from law to medicine . . . to business . . . to academics . . . to the arts . . . who are equally well informed on Jewish sources and who live by Jewish values.

We are thus committed to the future of a vigorous Jewish life in America, and we invite people not only from the community of Los Angeles but also from throughout the United States to join in this historic venture, which is already well on the way. Our present enrollment of Middle and Senior High School students totals 250. Before the end of the decade, we will grow to 650 students, filling our planned educational facilities.

Become a part of our MASTER PLAN while joining us for the reality of today . . . the reality of the students and parents who already call our Community High School "home."

I look forward to working together and learning together.

# RABBI ISAIAH ZELDIN

## PHILOSOPHY

Stephen S. Wise Community High School is dedicated to excellence in education, the continuity of the Jewish people, and the intellectual, emotional, social, creative, physical, and spiritual growth of each student. The school is committed to pluralism in Jewish religious practice, responsibility to the covenant between God and the Jewish people, and *Tikkun Olam*, the betterment of the world.

The School believes that a good education is one in which the unique gifts of each student are identified and nurtured. A good Jewish education provides meaning and purpose for those gifts, and a combination of secular knowledge and Jewish ideals creates competent people with moral vision.

The School believes that a rigorous college preparatory education is an essential tool for intelligent participation in the international exchange of ideas. A liberal arts course of studies develops confidence, encourages critical thinking, and nurtures creative expression.

The School's ultimate mission is the education of fully integrated human beings who offer to the world enlightened leadership in all areas of human endeavor, a leadership guided and informed by Jewish tradition and melded with the highest ideals of Western Civilization.

## IN THE BEGINNING,

The Following Members Met at Each Other's Homes With Isaiah and Florence Zeldin to Form a New Temple. We Decided in 1964 to Call the New Temple "Stephen S. Wise."

John and Susan Antignas

Clifford and Sydell Acheatel

Ethel Rosenberg Axelrad

Philip Rosenberg

Robert and Renee Bienenfeld

Alex and Helen Billens

Manny and Pearl Borinstein

Joe and Audrey Cahn

Arthur and Mandy Carmel

Renee Schutzbank Charney

Gerald Schutzbank

Lewis and Bette Chudd

Herbert and Harriett Citrin

Milton and Phyllis Cole

Sydney and Constance Dunitz

Gerald and Maxine Dunitz

Shirley Eichberg Greenes

Norman Eichberg

Irving Feintech

Norman and Evelyn Feintech

Richard and Ruth Felmus

Martin and Judith Freedman

Jerome and Miriam Heinrich

Howard and Ruth Helfman

Harry and Joan Helft

Abe and Sylvia Hershenson

Ben and Lynne Imershein

Bob and Lila Kadner

Joe and Shirley Kleinman

Paul and Sandy Krentzman

Andrew and Florence Lazar

Sid and Shirley Lockitch

Fred and Florence Plotkin

Julian and Ruth Pregulman

Irving and Minnie Prell

Donald and Lily Rosman

Merle and Dorothy Sharpe

Milton and Denalee Sheinbein

Leo and Gloria Stone

Harry and Florence Warner

David and Marilyn Williams

Ben and Elaine Winters

The Rest Is History

# About the Author

PAUL J. CITRIN IS a native of Los Angeles and a third-generation Californian. He was ordained a rabbi by the Hebrew Union College in 1973. In 1972, he studied modern Hebrew literature independently in Jerusalem. He graduated from U.C.L.A. with a Bachelor of Arts degree in history in 1968. The focus of his rabbinate has always been on congregational life. His passions are education, interfaith dialogue, Israel, and social justice. He co-founded the Jewish-Catholic Dialogue of Albuquerque, which expanded to include Protestants and Muslims. Rabbi Citrin also served on the board of the Dr. Martin Luther King Multi-Cultural Council, which provides college scholarships to minority students. He served as president of the Pacific Association of Reform Rabbis and as a board member of the Central Conference of American Rabbis. He is the author of two children's books, one a novel and one a prayer book for young people. He has written three books for adults on contemporary issues, Jewish theology, and a memoir on his own spiritual development. He is married to Susan Morrison Citrin. They have four children and eight grandchildren. Rabbi Citrin, retired in Albuquerque, continues to teach adults at a variety of venues in the state. Hiking, biking, writing, and travel are among his favorite celebrations.

# Sources

## INTERVIEWS

Metuka Benjamin Director of Education
Gray Davis, Former California Governor
Aviva Feintech, Advocate of the Parenting Center
Steven Fink, Past Temple President
Ken Gross, Past Temple President and interviewer of Shy
Eli Herscher, Senior Rabbi Emeritus and Shy's successor
Raz Husayni- Temple archives
Leah Kroll, Rabbi educator, and Shy's daughter-in-law
Nathan Lam, Senior Cantor of Stephen S. Wise Temple
Frank Ponder, a student of Shy and an active Temple member
Ellen Shumsky, a student of Shy
Leonard Thal, Retired Vice President of the URJ
David Woznica, Associate Rabbi at Wise Temple
Anita Zeldin, niece of Shy
Joel Zeldin Shy's elder son, attorney at law
Michael Zeldin Shy's younger son, a retired Professor of Education at Hebrew
    Union College, Los Angeles
Sivan A. Zakai PhD. Granddaughter of Shy, Professor of Education
Yoshi Zweiback, Senior Rabbi of Wise Temple
YouTube "Shabbat at Wendy's"

## ARCHIVAL MATERIAL, BOOKS & PERIODICALS

Leo Baeck, *The Essence of Judaism,* 1961.
Martin Buber collection of Hassidic stories
Stephen S. Wise Temple archives. Boxes 1–15
*Stephen S. Wise Temple High Holy Day Machzor*
Ian Russ Shabbat sermon in Tribute to Shy and the Temple Collection of
    Stephen S. Wise quotes

Sources

*Amarim.* Stephen S. Wise Temple monthly bulletins
Abba Hillel Silver, *Where Judaism Differed,* 1956.
Isaiah Zeldin. *Eighty-five Stories for Eight-Five Years,* 2005.
Isaiah Zeldin. *What This Modern Jew Believes,* 1996.
*The Jewish Journal,* Los Angeles
*Heritage,* an independent Jewish paper in Los Angeles
*The Los Angeles Times*
Shy's Grandchildren's Remembrances

www.ingramcontent.com/pod-product-compliance
Lightning Source LLC
Chambersburg PA
CBHW071838090426
42737CB00012B/2291